Accounting for

It shouldn'
to an Accountant

Accountant ends up travelling the world and accidentally discovers important stuff. These are the things you wouldn't necessarily get taught whilst studying business or accountancy, but probably ought to be.

To Ally,

Who has walked with me through it all.

Forgive me, and tell me again that it was worth it?

Andrew.

To Jordan & Joel,

Who have seen my successes and my failures.

Don't be scared to make mistakes, embrace adventure

Dad.

Stupid in Sierra Leone

"Stupid, stupid, this is such a stupid way to die" swimming back to the shore after a quick swim out to what looked like a really nearby island, I was impressed how calm I was, how much time seemed to slow down and how drowning like this would be monumentally stupid. How would my wife and boys cope, who would explain how I died? I was even congratulating myself at not swearing. I was also not scared at the thought of the actual fact of dying, although if the manner was going to be unpleasant, it would likely be quick. The congratulations about lack of swearing took place in-between frantic gasps for breath. I recall wondering what would be going through my mind at the precise moment, would I be consciously slipping into unconsciousness. "3-2-1 back in the room" how come I couldn't get any air in my lungs, I wasn't that unfit was I? Nope, no air coming down, no energy left for swimming. One last head down effort at front-crawling my way through several strong but panicked strokes left me precisely in the same spot.

One of my companions on the beach had seen my distress and was heading back out to me. Without realising, he'd taken a longer but calmer route to the beach and was having no trouble whatsoever! He came alongside me and I was able to rest my hand on his shoulder and tread water and catch my breath. I recall thinking that this was how I'd taught our youngest son to swim in Jamaica all those years ago; swim out, hand on daddy's shoulder, gradually take it off as confidence rose. We then swam back, crawled up the rocks and I tried my hardest not to collapse on the beach. My sixty-something year old companion then decided he'd not had enough exercise for the day and went for a jog along the sands. I confess to being less than gracious in my thoughts at that precise moment.

Our host and guide for the day then informed us that his mother in law and another companion had drowned on this same beach two years prior, so he never swam there anymore.

I'd been out to Freetown now for the third time, in my role as Head of Finance for a start-up Hydro Electricity Developer.

After returning from Switzerland in the summer of 2011, I'd received a call out of the blue from Lynn; his son and business partner were established in Mayfair, London, working on a large Hydro-Electricity project in Sierra Leone but having real trouble getting proper accounting help. He recommended me as being trustworthy and capable, but wanted to sound me out before talking to them. Coincidentally, since returning to the UK, our voluntary support funding was drying out quickly, and a few months of project accounting would mend the holes in the bucket. So I thought. I'd met Lynn briefly in Colorado a few years prior, discussed finances, competence and bringing business experience to bear in the development world over a brief coffee, but not had any contact since then. This role would, I would later realise, restore the very significant hole in my CV, and it would rescue my career.

In a bizarre coincidence, it was Lynn who had physically rescued me that day in Sierra Leone, having been there on a cultural investigation trip for Joule Africa. He was meeting with local villagers and establishing their cultural values, so that Joule Africa would be sensitive to both real and felt needs in any potential negotiations. We'd all been staying in the same Freetown guesthouse and his guide and host had invited me along to the beach that day too.

I felt out of place in Mayfair. Not for nothing is it the most expensive Monopoly property card. This felt so very different to our lives and experiences of the past few years. I'd not even worn a suit for five years. The interview went well I suppose, I'd not had one for a while, unless one counts the US Immigration Visa process, which wasn't a pleasant experience! They asked what sort of money I was looking for, and my reply brought concealed smiles. I carefully explained that I was committed to voluntary work, but their project fitted in to my development sphere and I could therefore commit to a few months.

I would sort out their historical finances and establish all the various systems and processes for what would be hopefully become a substantial international company. This would tide me over until Christmas of 2011 and give us a platform from which we could assess what this next season of our lives might look like.

They called me later that evening, said they could work with me and, by the way, they'd increase my salary request by more than a third! I'd quite underestimated the scale of London Accounting salaries, and my own worth.

Driving along the bumpy roads, on another day, with a different Non-Government Organisation (NGO), my passenger was talking about their cultural experiences in Sierra Leone. They'd been working for an International Relief & Development NGO and were having problems with people visiting their compound who were uninvited and/or hanging around not contributing to the work. This was also generating significant security issues for the single women in the compound. It is still the case that most development workers, and missionaries we'd come across, especially to the more inhospitable and dangerous places, were single women. To help counter this security issue, they'd instituted a policy of asking the security team to record who came in; using two columns, one for expats and one for locals. Every business, or compound in Sierra Leone, and many other African places for that matter, seems to require guards. Never mind the issues surrounding the fact that in the west we refer to ourselves overseas as "expats" whereas typically those coming to us we refer to as "immigrants"! They could then get a handle on who was coming and who had genuine business being there. This went on for a while before one of the Sierra Leone "Selone" staff got really rattled and asked why it was that all the foreigners were treated as experts and the locals were therefore less important, being unskilled and incompetent?! In an attempt to make the categorisation of visitors easier to handle, they'd actually asked for "expats" and "locals" but the sounding of "expat" was heard and interpreted locally as "expert". The only logical end result was a lot of very offended local workers feeling undervalued and discriminated against, reinforced every single time they came to work! Selone people are patient and long-suffering and it had taken a while until they could take the offence no longer and spoke up.

I'd gone from unpaid charity work, in countries such as Jamaica, India, Thailand, Malaysia, Malawi and even Burma, to the riches of Mayfair. That specific ground level simple cash management advice I'd been bringing to the so called developing world was actually the very thing that this Mayfair Company required.

At the very birth of an organisation, even one that will grow into the millions and potentially billions of dollars, it is simple basic and robust accounting systems that form the foundation of trustworthy finances. Who knew?

Turns out that pronunciation is actually important – Mum was right after all

A brief conversation with a stranger, or, Career Guidance

It's 1981 and apart from a drunken overnight cruise to Holland one night when I was seventeen, I'd never travelled further than the south of France with our pen-friend family.

I'd done the sensible thing of leaving school on a Friday and starting work as a trainee Accountant the following Monday; well the sensible thing when "A" levels are "dis-appointing" and University appears not to be viable option anyway. Somehow great mock exam grades didn't materialise into actual results and I now had to rely upon my natural charm and wits. Scary.

Much later in life I would learn that politicians have two significant areas they meddle in, education and health. This year, I would then discover, university places were being reduced, and guess what, exam grade bandings were changed. Well, that's the excuse I like to tell myself, to explain the sudden drop in my exam performance.

My Advanced "A" level choices were confined to Maths and anything not language related. Maths, I was informed, would be my first choice seeing as I wouldn't be attending University and needed to get a job. Anything else didn't really matter but Economics seemed likewise sensible, and would probably be useful someday. The school subject choice tables precluded taking both Maths and any language, and Physics was the least-worst option remaining. Not the cleverest planning. Languages were by far and away my easiest and most enjoyable subjects. However, my Career Guidance Counsellor impressed upon me that languages were useless in getting a job, unless one wanted to be an Interpreter in the EU. The process was little more than a three minute conversation, very one sided, and I confess to leaving feeling cheated. I failed Physics, and scraped passes at Economics and Maths. I ended up not liking School.

I'd written dozens of application letters for jobs and had just a few interviews. I'd even bought myself a smart suit from C&A. There was a promising position, or rather a likely job rather than an interesting role, at Lloyds in Chatham. I'd apparently done well at this interview and the job (paying £2,200 pa) was essentially policy checking for Lloyds Insurance policies. That's it, spell checking, all day every day. One evening my Father came back in from work, with an application form for a Trainee Accountant at Abbott Laboratories on the Isle of Sheppey. I am still unsure what he, as a Police Officer, was doing at a Pharmaceutical company. Anyway, I completed the form and sent it in. Neatly circumventing the entire application process, my form stood out and I secured an interview. Amazingly, I was offered that job too. It paid £3,300 pa and promised training. I took the Abbott role.

Looking back at my life several decades later, it is amazing to see that the things I valued at eighteen are still important to me now. I loved, but didn't know it yet or was unable to articulate it, languages and cultures. I also loved tennis and wouldn't realise until years later that even slightly above average ability in this sport would open doors to people and experiences all over the world. I was pretty good at Maths, despite my A level score, having taken my GCSE a year early for example. I'd learn that numbers come through as a language all of their own, even if at a practical level all this means is simply that you can make sense of numbers when others cannot.

If you don't plan, you'll end up going where the current takes you

Healthcare is good business, people equals healthcare

Working in the very large Accounts dept. of a major pharmaceutical company in the south of England, I began to see my life slowly panning out before me. It didn't look exciting. It looked even less exciting when I was told that once I'd learned the intricacies of "export costing and variance analysis", yes that was the job, I'd be ready in a year or two to start looking at different aspects of the dept. An accounting qualification and a decent position were mine for the taking, if I could put in five years or more for the qualifications and a further five years to get the relevant experience in each function. This might appeal to some, and indeed this would be a great position for those seeking stability, comfort and routine. Not me.

On my first day, I found myself on the sea defences that bordered the manufacturing site, having a calming cigarette. There was another first day gent too, Ray. He was going to work in the Export dept., having had a varied international career. Mysterious and tough, he had the air of maybe a much more colourful life! Somehow we became friends. Two years later, and Ray was the only friend who told me not to marry my fiancée, he didn't trust her eyes. My marriage lasted two weeks, apparently she had been having an affair with a work colleague during the engagement.

For younger readers, back in 1981, computers were in gas filled clean rooms and there was a single printer for the entire company. The Accounts team had fifty members. Getting your team's reports off the only printer on site involved chatting up the Lady in charge of the Computer Suite. This was a basic necessity of working life. I was youngest and prettiest and so this became my daily walk.

A Personal Computer (PC) was mysteriously introduced into its own nook, and we were allowed to book an hour a week to see whether it could in fact be made to do anything useful.

Most of my accounting co-workers were male; just one lady in the entire dept. Dress code in the 1980s was a lot less conservative let's say, I recall one day her blouse was so low cut a boob fell out and was resting on the desk. I wore a grey three piece suit, with my grandfather's demob pocket watch. The suit's colour matched the role.

There were plenty of strong characters on the large site. Basic manners and decent behaviour are less evident than one might think and I had a good reputation with other staff. Politeness is a basic value, it's a choice really, and indeed doesn't cost anything.

My immediate boss asked me to write up a report on variances one particular month. He then took great perverse delight in telling me that he'd then re-written it in his own hand and presented it as his own work and had been commended for it. I smiled.

After eighteen months I left, deciding that bluffing my way into a better paid and more senior job would be so much quicker than waiting around for multiple indeterminate years in the current one.

Everyone is weird, including you!

Your best chance of a pay rise is to switch jobs and aim up

My next job was working for an importer of potato starch; I'm not making these jobs up, they exist. It's in most foodstuffs and is the base component of wallpaper paste, so now you know. I was now the Assistant Accountant, exploring the world of accruals and prepayments, imprest systems and Director's drawings. Not the artistic kind, except when reading what he claimed he'd spent on business. A close working proximity with the front loading computer main-frame was a daily highlight – seriously – taking out large reels of magnetic tape and loading them up onto the front of the Joe-90 contraption. If you google ® the Joe-90 opening scenes, I think it's worth it.

Most of my co-workers were female and this brought its own learning experience. Every day began with a chat about their relationships, home life, children, other halves and work only started afterwards. They were complicated. Work processes were regimented, ordered and straightforward, once learned. The challenge therefore was navigating the people, not the job. There were ping-pong memo sheets that had to be responded to by writing on the carbon paper behind the original message, E-mail had not yet been invented of course. Accounting seemed to be all about getting the data in, rather than working out what it all meant.

I saw the real life impact of drink and its impact on an alcoholic co-worker. The jokes on TV and the stereotypes one sees on this subject, are real. The Company Secretary, who ran the daily operations in place of the Managing Director (MD), was this man. He could be nasty and snide to those beneath him. This was not only in organisational hierarchy, but also in his view of their status and value, relative to him, when sober. I think because I was such a junior, and likely not to be a threat, he was never unpleasant towards me. That didn't mean I wasn't slightly fearful every time I walked into his office, that I'd be the one on the end of his sarcasm and bile. I saw the "morning after" impact on skin, clothes and breathe. I have learned, as I've aged, that alcohol tends to exacerbate ones already-there character attributes. He also used to drive to the pub every lunch time.

This really was a different age. There was a need for the Jimmy Saville "clunk click" adverts on TV, and "don't drink and drive" specials, precisely because my boss' actions were not uncommon. They also tended to be accepted, much as smoking in the work place! Different times, and not as long ago as you might think.

As wise as we believe ourselves to be, today, that wisdom was not there for 99.9% of man's history.

I lasted about eighteen months, again. The failed marriage to a co-worker spurred on the job hunting this time around. There were similarly paid jobs around aplenty, but the pay appropriate to slightly more senior and qualified positions was in some cases half as much again or more. So started my first ever Curriculum Vitae or CV. I only got a single A grade in my GCSE Ordinary levels (you might need to google that too if you're under 50), in English. I put that skill to good use.

I would in later years come to realise that the only reason I was able to turn up on time for work that season, was my Mum would call me in the mornings! I did apologies, several times, in later life as I began to become more self-aware. In hind-sight, I could have gone for a job that started later!

You have a few weeks in your new job to live up to the expectations you created in your interview! Use that time wisely.

Oh yes, you have to get along with your co-workers, not like them.

Never trust a prospective employer who invites you to the interview at a hotel

I must confess, a fifty per cent pay rise and a company car was a real attraction. The warning signs were everywhere during the interview, and I steadfastly managed to ignore all of them – after all, there was a company car, which I was assured would be "any two litre car you wanted". The car was the deal clincher for me; early twenties and the chance of finally driving something quality simply too tempting.

This was for a group of companies in the Motor Trade Refinishing Supplies business, with what I found later, was a Head office literally under the railway arches in Peckham. Think Del Boy and Only Fools and Horses but a lot less charming. My own office was a shared attic room above a paint and body panel supply shop – I'd never before encountered migraines, but it's amazing what a powerful effect hundreds of litres of paint fumes has on the brain.

It was a group with nine companies, all mostly doing the same thing and each run by a family member or friend. I was invited to a golf day once, but not being considered good enough to play, I was only there to bring the cash to pay for the event! Mule? The other notable work event was a night out at Brighton Dogs. Now, I'm not being classist, but it opened up an area of society I'd not seen too much of before, even though I'd managed to spend most nights down the pub during my teens.

Computers and PCs were just being rolled out. Being the eighties, we had a flashy salesperson roll up in his three litre Capri and – I kid you not – produce a quote on the back of a packet of Silk Cut Cigarettes. Its packaging was mainly white. The salesman and the company directors all thought this was a real hoot. I recall being distinctly unimpressed, but it wasn't my money it was theirs.

My job would be to install the spanking new accounting software package on a new PC in each of the nine branches. What could possibly go wrong with that?

Apart from being telephoned each morning by the owner demanding to know what the f*** I was doing with his money – the work was relatively easy. I made it look that way but after bluffing my way into the role at the interview, by promising efficient ways of producing meaningful group reports. It did have me inwardly sweating, it's easy and quick to blag at interview but I was now having to back myself up. The daily abuse and work patterns did nothing to lessen my nervousness over the time I spent there.

Their stand out best salesperson was this vague swaggering chap, I don't think I ever spoke with him, but he worked out of the Arches, Peckham. I then heard one week of his sacking. He'd been pocketing cash along the way of taking orders and receiving payments. Wow, I thought, brave man. He was then re-employed a couple of weeks later, apparently the company sales dropped so substantially, it was worth the cash incentives to keep the sales up!

My choice of company car was replaced with the owners wife's clapped out Ford Capri within five minutes of starting. Basically the main benefit of taking the job removed in an instant. This was a sign of things to come it turned out.

Holidays, apparently, were not allowed to be taken, and just fifteen days were standard in this industry anyway, until after you'd been employed for a full year. My every movement appeared to be monitored. Looking back it reminds me of the film "The Firm" but with a "sauf eas London innit" feel.

One stand out memory of this time was driving back home from Brixton through the London traffic on a Friday night and stopping by the gutter to puke my guts out – a seriously bad migraine caused by yet another day in a paint fume filled office. I arrived home around seven o'clock, literally fell on the bed in my suit and woke up around eight. Not feeling quite right, I went downstairs and switched on the TV to see Noel's House Party – I'd managed to sleep for twenty five hours without moving.

A couple of branches in Wales meant five am starts and an abusive phone call half way down the M4 checking whether I would be on time. On the up-side, this kept me from nodding off on more than one occasion though.

I discovered, or was confronted with the fact, that some of the Welsh disliked the English, rather openly and with a passion. I thought we were all one big happy "nation". I was quite wrong. I felt very naïve, why didn't I know this stuff?

Another branch, in south east London, was run by a likeable character, always surrounded by pretty young ladies. His was my favourite branch to visit, although I always felt a little like the lost new boy. He told me one day quite casually that he earned his real pocket money at the weekend by running cash around for Arms Dealers.

Computerising their particular accounting was causing a few problems for me. The numbers didn't add up, and then patterns started to materialise which were odd. Another quite casual chat with the very likeable Manager revealed that a major "alternative accounting process" had been going on for years and would I be able to make the computer system "cope" with it. The little business model that they'd been working was one where if it stopped, it would be discovered. Everyone wanted it to continue, of course. The trouble was, with double entry book-keeping and computerised accounting, that stuff gets very difficult indeed to tuck away. I was very young, innocent, and scared; I fudged the issue, resolving to get myself out of there as soon as I could.

I then had my first ever disciplinary chat and a verbal warning with the Marketing Director, the son-in-law of the owner, who was too cross to talk to me, about how if I knew what was good for me I'd get on and fix the computer system to properly and "appropriately" record what was going on. I said to him that it was illegal and would lose me my accounting qualifications, not to mention possible prison, to no avail. He persisted with the line that it would be in my best interests to find a way I could be happy with and get it done…

Suddenly, I bravely decided that a new career opportunity beckoned. It was really tough to get to interviews when you couldn't take any time off and were followed around by the owner wanting to swear at you all the time!

I decided that this was a learning experience and, having survived it, I'd be much wiser in the future. I'd really nail them down on the company car details in the interview for sure next time.

Talking about survival does remind me of my proper first near-death experience. Having bought a house that needed renovation, I was left with a simple job of drilling holes in which to place wall sockets. There was, so I was informed, a single live input, to which the drill was connected and everything was dead. It took about a millisecond for my drill to connect with an old cable, immediately followed by a loud bang, a blue flash and I came to against the opposite wall having been thrown back! Oh how we laughed…

I may have an Achilles heel when it comes to cars. It took until I was into my forties to finally grow up with regards to cars and status and self-worth and all that. In case you are wondering, I currently drive a nineteen year old battered Renault that cost me £100.

I refer to this time in on my CV as "character building"

The company no longer exists, it went bankrupt a few years later

It really is all about who you know

People employ you, people give you pay rises, people reward you.

I started off in my professional life just trying to get on with people. Some of this is due to my personality style, which abhors conflict. Somewhere along the way I learned that if you ask people open ended questions, you have to talk less yourself. There's then less chance of people thinking you are stupid or not worth knowing! However, asking people about themselves gets them talking and this seems to almost universally help establishing a relationship. They end up thinking you are really nice, and all you've done is listened, this in itself signifies value in them. Time is value.

I finally landed an interview for an Estate Agency Chain, Prudential Property Services (PPS). They were fast growing through acquisition and were recruiting for a Management Accountant. I requested a late (after six) interview slot so as to avoid being followed by the previous nutters. This, by itself, should have been a warning that any stated contractual working hours mean nothing for Accountants.

There were now local offices and no early starts into rioting Brixton, neither an abusive Peckham Boss nor racist Welsh Managers. It all appealed greatly. Another pay rise, a car plus a decent pension were a bonus. The Finance Director (FD) interviewing took one look at my CV and saw that we'd both worked at the same Starch Importers and proceeded to chat about all the staff he knew and how they were getting on. After about fifty five minutes of this, he asked me five minutes' worth of questions and the job was mine.

I did promise that implementing budgeting and management reporting on their brand new PCs and Spread-sheets would be a piece of cake... not having ever used a Spread-sheet package before!

Blagging sort of came with the territory by now; the irony of an Accountant moving from the Motor Trade to the Estate Agency Business wasn't lost on me.

I had a whole two weeks of working on preparing a basic budget model for the company. Fortunately, they'd not had any such budgets before. When I arrived the PC was still boxed and the "Smart" software package was shrink-wrapped. Nobody had used it, much less knew what it could do, and essentially anything I produced generated exclamations of "ooh wow that's amazing" as in the mini monsters in Toy Story. My best job so far by a long way.

Looking for green field accounting positions should be high on anyone's career plan. Anything you do is brilliant; there was nothing before so it's all an improvement. Also, you then become the expert! Experts get paid more.

The Estate Agency chain went from twenty five branches to three hundred and fifty over the next couple of years. Being well placed and regarded always counts well when growth is happening. I ended up being the Financial Accountant, reporting to the FD, managing a team of over twenty and driving decent company cars. Back in the days when car tax was based on engine size, with 1400cc being the cut off point for the lowest rate, the Renault 5GT Turbo was a brilliant toy. I mean it was a useful and economic business tool for visiting the various regional offices and Directors.

Along with the perks comes the responsibility, I eventually found out. As the pay increases, so the hours become longer and longer. I would frequently be the last person out and have to set the alarms. We Accountants also have our own "time of the month". The month-end process can only be started once the period is over, takes a week and you are always somehow feeling like you are never on top of the workload. Dealing with staff was a shock too. Confrontation didn't come easily and therefore presented me with some emotional challenges along the way. The way I handled conflict was to take everything back to the facts and remove the emotion. One painful encounter now would prevent many more from ever happening.

Don't trust Management Consultants. The basic premise seemed to be, apart from having a flashy looking piece of software on an expensive laptop, which had just been invented, to ask all the staff what needed fixing and how to fix it and then re-write all that into a report and deliver it as though it's your own work. In reality, senior and middle management often instinctively know what needs to be done, but are rarely asked. Sometimes management Consultants are brought in so as to take the blame for the unpopular decisions about to be made. My opinion.

Fax machines were invented, destroying at a stroke the excuse "it's in the post". Jules Verne foresaw these a century before by the way. This phrase was a lovely convenience and both giver and receiver knew what it meant. It was an interlude during which the thing that had been promised would eventually get taken care of, with some leeway recognising that the deliverer wasn't always in full control of events!

Five years with the Prudential ended abruptly; the end of mortgage tax relief created a property slide and implosion of the business model. We'd been warning of this for a while, but communication with the Head Office MD was only one way, and it wasn't up. The real business model, and why Prudential had bought the estate agency chains in the first place, was the ability to sell mortgage and insurance products to house movers. Our regional group was cut down to a hundred offices and finally sold to a guy who had a small chain of Launderettes. He then sold many of the original Partnership offices back to their former owners. They had all been paid substantial amounts from the Prudential in the first place and were now much happier, and richer!

Redundancy and the manner of it, was still a surprise. Trusting and still a little naïve, I vaguely wondered why my London based Head of Finance was spending more and more time in our office. That became clear when he moved into my position as soon as I was made redundant. There was also the letter I was required to sign before they would release a cheque to me for my notice. I obviously wasn't aware of my employment rights, but things were different then, the power definitely didn't sit with the employee. The timing, not that there's a good time for these things, was just a few weeks before my wedding.

I went from a £30,000 Rover to a £30 push bike overnight. Many philosophies and much religious thought suggest if you can learn to be happy whatever your circumstances, life is so much easier! I went through a very quick personal assessment in this regard and decided that "stuff" wasn't what defined me or determined my happiness. That process itself was priceless and has been of lifelong benefit.

Sod the kitchen and bathroom. It was fun to take my redundancy, visit the high street travel agent and ask what the best Honeymoon location was. I was pointed in the direction of the Caribbean and booked a five star hotel in St Lucia over Christmas and the New Year. It still reaps benefits in my marriage twenty five years later. Inspired.

I had another near-death encounter on our honeymoon, which Mrs M did not find at all funny. Why wind-surf where everyone else is going? Well, so you don't get dragged out to sea and dangerous rocks and have to be rescued is why!

I worked there for five years and didn't think much about pensions, but being an insurance company, they were generous. Now into my fifties, this is by far the biggest part of my, optimistically described, pension plan. Compound returns over three decades and almost by accident I have something that is large enough to be meaningful.

Starting a pension plan early is wisdom indeed

Do your homework before you drive two hours for interview?

Arguing with Recruitment Consultants, another classy Business, alongside Motor Trade and Estate Agency, at least means they'll remember you when something interesting comes up.

Yes, I'd so far managed to combine the fine art of accounting, which has been referred to as "cooking the books" by some, together with Estate Agents and the back-street Auto trade, classy.

The "Consultant" was some girl even younger than me who saw it as her role to advise me on how to progress my career, by taking any offer of an interview she suggested. She wasn't overly happy with my CV. I said I wouldn't change it and she said I'd be unemployable. Literally a couple of days later she called me to say a perfect position had come up and didn't I have just the perfect CV to send off to them and wasn't she clever.

If you're wondering about my arrogant stand, I'd simply put some personal interest and value statements at the bottom of the CV. Hardly career limiting IMO. To my mind technical ability ought to be the same across all professionals applying for jobs, and just maybe what people were also looking for was character and personality. The company happened to be a US Music publisher based in the US with a small UK office looking after European sales. The recruitment consultant happily took credit for matching up my perfect CV to the prospective employer.

The Consultant forgot to mention, as did the employer, and I didn't even think to ask, that it was a temporary role covering maternity leave. Note to self, don't make that mistake again! I still didn't discover this until turning up, after a two hour drive, for the interview. It paid half of what I was earning before, but it was on the sunshine coast, and at least it was a job before the wedding. I was able to get married "employed". I'd sort out whether it was just for a few months at a later time. Thankfully, on the first day, commencing the handover process with an obviously pregnant incumbent, she said she had no intention of coming back! And so a temporary role became a five year position.

One really appealing aspect to me of the interview was the fact that the US parent company wanted periodic visits to sort out budgets and reporting. Part of the interview had been conducted over the phone with the US Finance Director. (This was in the days before Skype)

I managed to encourage my UK Managing Director that he'd need me with him to talk through the budgets in detail. Totally true by the way, details escaped him, he just needed my encouragement to fully realise it!

This would then start my passion for places, people and cultures not my own. I discovered I loved travelling, and some companies would even pay you to do it.

Every new role would now have to have an overseas element.

America feels familiar; we watch the programmes, laugh at the comedy and "get" the nuances don't we? The reality was very different indeed. I actually found myself struggling to ask for milk in my tea in Alabama, somehow having to find several inflections in the word "milk" before I was understood.

Drinking is not just a responsible choice, it's a cultural thing with consequences and meaning all on its own. Other cultures have varying degrees of tolerance and implied value when it comes to alcohol. I was simply unaware and assumed everybody is like "us".

Several of us had gone out to lunch with one of the directors to a restaurant and along with the meal I ordered a small beer. Things went really quiet and then this director said quite calmly that "we" didn't drink and I needed to order a soft drink. There's a part of me that wanted to assert my right to have a drink with my lunch if I wanted to, but part of me also knew that I'd be sacked immediately if I dared to challenge his authority in any way. He didn't directly employ me, but I knew I'd last about as long as it took to make a phone call on the way back to the office.

I managed to slowly learn the little rules that governed southern US management practice, mostly painlessly, by watching others get caught out. Informal gets formalised, authority is all. A lot of this is summarised by "at will" employment contracts; you are employed "at the will or whim" of your employer and can then be sacked at any time for no or any reason. This then helps explain why US Drama shows always seem to have people working all hours and holidays and generally in fear of losing their jobs. They are.

To counter the negative leadership experience of earlier jobs, I was rewarded with a great role model in the shape of our South African / Australian international Vice President (VP). Having lived life "fully" when he was young and in a band, he now for example disciplined himself by fasting on Mondays. He was the archetypal cool-under-pressure-never-flustered manager. Contrary to most South Africans and Australians I have ever met since, who are all, so far as I can tell, quite happily bonkers.

We heard a story from one of our European distributors. As the Russian and Eastern-bloc former Iron-Curtain countries opened up for trade, a friend of his was invited to show his good faith in a potential business deal by bringing $2,000 in cash with him in his briefcase. He was shot and his briefcase taken.

I learned that week-end accommodation and flights are cheaper than week-days. Tourists will pay less than business travellers, who are not spending their own money. I then managed to convince my boss that if I booked a week-end flight, I could bring my Mrs M along and still end up saving money for the company. Now this doesn't always work but it did for two US trips paid for entirely by the company!

I also discovered that flying through so called gateway cities meant you could stop over for a day or two for no extra cost and visit lots of cool places. I went to New Orleans, Atlanta, Orlando and Cincinnati on the way back from Alabama.

England's a cool place ethnically and racially. Whatever issues we might have, we are way ahead of the United States. I decided to do the European or British thing of taking the metro from my Atlanta hotel to the CNN Tower. Only later did I understand people's real surprise at this; I found myself possibly the only white face underground. I figured everyone else assumed I was a tourist, felt sorry for me and so left me alone. I later heard my colleague talk of walking around the corner to see someone laying on the ground in front of him having been shot just moments earlier.

It was an issue for quite a while, for our young sons, as to why we went to Disney without them! We had shown them our pictures from the US Trips, before they were born, and they really couldn't get their heads around it.

Americans value loyalty and deference rather too highly

And so to my second disciplinary event. My first of course being refusing to participate in a fraud. My British boss was fond of saying whatever he thought the US guys wanted to hear; "sure we'll get a 5% response rate on this marketing plan" for example, when every one of the previous dozen had elicited barely 2%. I had therefore got a little used to managing his forecasts down to more realistic numbers. From a personal point of view, it was me that would be hauled up in front of everyone to embarrassingly explain why we were missing budget again.

This particular evening, not only had he failed to mention to the US CEO that the marketing list we were buying was one he personally had a stake in, but also that his assumption of a 5% hit rate was double all the recent history. Without really thinking, I adjusted the figures down slightly and presented the numbers later.

To my surprise I found myself at the end of a disciplinary discussion about subverting the authority of a direct instruction from my superior, delivered from my British boss, whose ass I was trying to save, on behalf of the US director and owner. The fact that every forecast he'd delivered always substantially underperformed was irrelevant in the context of the subordinate accountant undermining his authority. My job, apparently, was to present the numbers knowing them to be totally spurious?!

Interesting legal point; in the US, a lawyer can represent you even if they know you to be guilty whereas in the UK, they cannot.

The solution, of course, was as simple as telling the story but crucially ascribing the true credit to all estimates! I know that now of course, being older and wiser. Let them know who made the estimates and what assumptions have been made, by whom, to get to the bottom line.

Aspiring Accountants, learn to quote your source!

Living on the coast, I had the sea to play with. I went off windsurfing again, tried showing off to my father-in-law, as only blokes do, and had to be rescued yet another time. I'd made it a very long way out this occasion and was simply too exhausted to hold on anymore!

This same UK boss, thanks to the six hour time zone difference, spent a season of mornings at home building his extension before turning up to the office a few minutes before the US office came online, and giving the impression of being hard at work all day. Now, in hindsight, he may have had permission to do this, I doubt it though. One of my colleagues decided to let the US CEO in on this. The response was immediate and harsh, she was given a stern rebuke and official warning by the jobbing builder less than an hour later. Loyalty to authority seemed, in this company at least, a much stronger held value than only working in the afternoons apparently.

The US Company went for a public listing on the stock market. As junior Accountants, we get used to understanding numbers, seeing threats and risks and then, sometimes, never getting the opportunity to share it all! Chasing the investor dollar was not such a cool idea. I instinctively felt that control would be lost and so too the motivation for all they did.

The company was relatively small and owned by friends. They had full creative control and could indulge in pet projects, doing what they wanted, when they wanted. The plan though was to go public. This would open up investment, and returns. It was their chance to fulfil the American dream. They'd all become substantially richer in the process. They eventually managed a listing. But from then on, everything they did appeared to be for the benefit of the market analysts. Keeping these commentators happy was the key to maintaining the share price. The company became about the stock, not music, they had lost their soul. I'm convinced this was part of what lead to their eventual demise and the selling of its back catalogue a few years later.

I had received an assurance of sorts from my UK boss that when he moved on, I'd be up for the job. In the end however, they employed someone I found it increasingly hard to work with. After being there for five years, I could see no growth or change; my career was parked in neutral. I decided it was time to move on. I would only later recognise the benefits of working in an easy job just a ten minute drive from home. I had taken for granted the ability to pop home for an hour around five o'clock to see my young son, and then pop back again to the office in the evening to finish the tasks of the day.

There comes a point, I think in all careers, where choices need to be made; having your cake and eating it is indeed a truism. I was bored and frustrated with this job, but around for family and leisure. Did I actually ask myself "which is better"? I don't think I did. Maybe it's all seasonal, maybe the grass always looks greener.

Ask yourself about the values that drive a company

A foreign language means a higher salary

After five years in the music industry, as much as it provided a safe and easy job with family friendly working hours, I was bored. It was never going to get better or bigger. I was going to stay there until whenever, or, move on again for pastures new.

Deliberately now looking for jobs with an overseas connection, I happened upon a data management company. They were advertising for an internationally aware accountant and mentioned that they'd been recently acquired by a French oil company. My recruitment consultant friend, who himself ended up a director of a FTSE100 company, said I'd never get anywhere close to getting the job. My CV and most recent experience was simply too weak. He was entirely correct of course.

Ignoring his well-intentioned professional opinion, I went for it.

Bob Monkhouse's condensed wisdom on public speaking is essentially to pretend to be the person they are expecting to see. Then you are simply confirming in their minds you are the right person for the speech, presentation, project, or indeed job. The other comment that stuck with me is that in most "performance situations", they want you to succeed. You failing would be awful and embarrassing, for everyone in the room. Technical competence is almost always assumed, taken from your CV, otherwise you wouldn't be in the room at all. Your job at interview is to convince them then that you are indeed exactly the individual they've been looking for.

Bob Monkhouse made much of his money from coaching business leaders in public speaking. It's simply acting using words. Most of his clients, some household names, were just pretending to be Titans of Industry and as scared of public speaking as the rest of us. Acting.

The pay was half as much again as I'd been earning; there was insurance, pension and a car. Soon into the interview I was asked whether I thought I was worth being paid such a high salary – "absolutely" was my immediate but measured and steely eyed reply.

I may have slightly over-estimated my then ability to converse in French. Fortunately for me, my interviewer didn't speak French at all.

We copied, stored and analysed historic and current oil exploration data for larger oil companies, in our case a French oil exploration company. Lots of this oil-field data was created in the boom of the 1960s and 1970s and stored on magnetic tapes. Some thirty years on, it was discovered that oil fields move, and therefore change shape, when you suck the oil out. By studying the historic data alongside the current data you could increase oil field life by 30%. This was a hugely beneficial discovery. The only problem with this is that all the computers able to read the historic data were obsolete, having last been used several decades ago. We had managed to convert a couple of old machines to read the data across onto new ones, and then convert this data into modern storage mediums. This started a process of going round the world to old African and former Communist countries who might still have some of this old kit laying around and buying them up!

Having blagged the job, again, I now needed to win over the accounting team. My view on this is that it means being able to join them in their tasks, showing them that you know how to do their jobs and are indeed willing on occasion to knuckle down and do it with them. It also means making your share of teas and coffees and remembering to bring in cakes from time to time! The occasional early finish for a job well done hardly hinders relations either.

Winning my boss over was harder. This young and bright FD probably spoke French as well as I did, but didn't have my possibly misplaced confidence, or general lack of awareness of the consequences, to try!

I took over responsibility for the accounting software, and oversaw subsidiary finances in the USA as well as in Africa and the Middle East. I was going to do the more adventurous subsidiaries also, but these at the time meant bullet proof vests, private security teams and bomb proof cars. I was happy, at the time, to let my boss volunteer for those assignments! Looking back now, I might have enjoyed these assignments maybe even more.

Having boldly declared my ability in all these areas, I had to deliver; it did mean long hours and brushing up my French and getting out of my comfort zone. Fortunately, most accounting packages are much the same. Most subsidiaries have the same issues. Most Accountants have the same problems to resolve. My real struggle was speaking French in a business context when my colleagues spoke no English!

I found that under duress, I could force the concentration for a couple of hours and so I learned to structure my monthly Paris meetings so that French-only meetings took place in the mornings and English meetings in the afternoons. I was pretty good at French at school but the real benefit was in hindsight the summer holidays I spent with a French exchange family as a young teenager. I was really grateful to my parents for that opportunity.

Blagging always requires you to make good on your promises

Thinking back to the monthly commute to Paris, I'm reminded of the day that someone before me sent their bag through the x-ray machine and forgot to collect it the other side. We were all evacuated back into the terminal as they took the now suspicious case away to deal with. After a while we heard a very large bang as they performed a controlled explosion. A few minutes later a very sheepish lady was escorted through the terminal with the mangled remains of her overnight case pushed along by airport security.

The group Finance Director (FD) came into town for his monthly visit. With my own FD by now out of the picture, I was acting FD and although technically I ought to have been paid for this I wasn't. I was therefore in the hot seat for the morning. I'd prepared thoroughly of course. What surprised and impressed me was that he only brought with him a single sheet of paper, our balance sheet.

He would start by taking an item, like debtors, and then just asking me about that number. My answers, the level of detail, confidence and ability to tell a story, all told him whether we were managing debtors or not. It was almost like the bigger the number on the balance sheet, the less numbers he wanted and the more narrative, or storytelling, he looked for.

Additional questions would then lead to a position of confidence, or not, with this particular subsidiary. Impressive. Simple.

That is how you manage a billion dollar company

The company had a stringently enforced no-swearing culture. On one occasion a staff member was invited to go home and consider what they'd done and how they could better fit in as a team player. It had seemed, to me, like he got rewarded, but in fact the culture was so strong that no one envied his early afternoon departure.

However, they were slightly lax in other areas. I discovered that we'd bought a £100,000 bomb proof car for our team in North Africa but that they were somehow unable to have it located. In the end, our Auditors were satisfied with emails from their manager that it was there and a photograph of the car on the quayside. I recall hearing that the car ended up with the Minister-for-something-or-other.

There was a mysterious older guy in Paris, who had an office and a desk, but the only one I observed to be devoid of a PC or terminal. I was told he travelled the world with a brown paper bag. I may have misheard, but allegedly, scholarships to significant international learning institutions and such like was where some of it got spent. So I was told, or vaguely recall, did I say allegedly? Let's just say that was a funny story they liked to tell against a much loved co-worker.

A government Minister of the African country came to the UK to perform an Audit. We'd only issued two invoices in the year. This became an object lesson in role creation and a master-class in how to spin a ten minute check into a four hour exercise. I still have no idea how he did it. The Minister and the Auditor, accompanied by wives for this business ~~shopping~~ trip, came to the office as they were required to audit the UK side of the paper-trail for the invoices we'd raised. He went from one piece of paper to another piece, checked payments, checked orders, double checked everything, again and then again, and strung it out for a happy few hours. Wonderful and bizarre. Then they all went shopping and saw a show. Businesses can use per-diems as a way of helping visitors to "manage" their time in London. This was what I was told.

Corporate culture is a real thing

Y2K happened

Millions of hours and countless resources were thrown at it. At our company it was the entire focus for most of the year. Elsewhere, everywhere, planes were grounded, and others, from memory in China, forced to fly with the IT specialists on board whilst the clocks ticked their way from 11:59 through 00:01. I think a clock in Cambridge stopped ticking and a few toasters didn't turn the bread brown.

Creative auditing

Another occasion and our Auditors wanted to know what had happened to a substantial amount of cash we'd wired down to our office. This was the same office in northern Africa. I persuaded our Auditors that a photo of our local manager, with a dated newspaper, standing in front of an open safe stacked high with the currency would suffice. The local manager thought it funny to stand in front with a cardboard cut-out of a Kalashnikov.

With the project eventually not being awarded, getting the cash out of the country was an issue. I suggested they buy a boat and sail it out. By the time I left, I heard that the cash had all been mislaid. I don't know whether this was in the same manner as the bomb-proof car. I may have been a little naïve in helping us pass a clean audit.

Embrace the crazy; horses, Japanese tourists, Venus and Mars

I spent a few evenings whilst in Egypt with the local manager, a nice chap who got the project posting out of the UK office and was loving the life! The Cairo thing to do, apparently, is to lease a horse much the same way one would lease a sports car, and go riding in the desert. Deciding to embrace the bizarre, I agreed and looked forward to an evening ride. Arabian horses are much thinner than British ones, making for a slightly uncomfortable perch. They even know their master's whistle too! The stables, if this could get any more surreal, were directly in front of the three main Cairo pyramids. Enjoying the experience of riding Arabian horses out in the desert in front of the pyramids I then took a call from the UK office; not telling them where I was just made the conversation all the more fun.

Another evening, they dropped me off in front of the Sphinx for a world-renowned laser light show and commentary on the pyramids, Egyptian history and mythology. Unfortunately, they got the wrong time and the taxi dropped me off just before the last show of the night, in Japanese. I'm sure the handful of Japanese tourists in the front row were bemused at me sitting a few rows behind them. That was truly a weird evening. The night sky was amazing, lasers pretty cool and soundtrack bizarre and to my ears, all so funny.

The final treat was an evening ride on a felucca, with a picnic, drifting down the Nile under starlight. In the sky and first to appear was Venus, so bright it was like the some giant was shining a torch out of the heavens. The last time Venus was this bright and this close, was apparently 2,000 years ago. Next to appear was Mars, completely and easily visible to the naked eye.

These experiences made me think about other cultures in a much more desirable way, along with simply going with the flow and seeing what happened. Choosing not to stress, whilst not taking, to my mind at least, unnecessary risks, now sounded like a worthy life choice.

So, looking forward to my next trip, a country in the middle of Africa.

I immediately doubted the wisdom espoused in previous paragraph.

The only anti-malarial effective in the region I was going to was Larium. The chemist, rather nonchalantly, warned of occasional side effects such as dreams and mental problems. There has been lots of media interest recently with soldiers attempting to sue the Ministry of Defence for insisting that Larium was routinely handed out to Army personnel and the long term mental health impacts now being realised. I had the weirdest dreams ever, bizarre, scary, and not all healthy. But I didn't catch Malaria, hey.

Having taken the principled stand not to pay any unusual tips I found myself at the front of the immigration queue, for an hour, whilst all those standing behind me were called forward for processing. My principals so far intact, didn't feel much like success. The airport carousel was broken and I got to see the unedifying sight of hundreds of cases all thrown in one huge pile, and then various crazy people climbing over each other to get to the top of the heap to find theirs. I decided patience would serve me well and waited for the crowds to subside before finding my own case.

I saw a machine gun wielding, literally hopping mad, Policeman stop traffic and shove his gun through the window of a perceived errant motorist.

I learned that one African value on display most of the time, was a lack of consideration towards the future. Hence people standing on the outside of VW Buses on bumpers and so on going sixty miles an hour down the bumpy roads. A friend described the different approach to time in the following way; Africans would sit on a train looking backwards, to history and to ancestors, whereas Westerners would sit looking forwards, to what was to come. Too simplistic?

Arrived at the second, guarded, company house in another City, just after someone had climbed the wall and let off both barrels of their shotgun through my bedroom window. Told to stay indoors Saturday morning, as they were parading thieves naked through the market and would be chopping off hands to stop them doing it again. They explained that everyone would be excitable and it would be much better all-round not to be out.

An interesting old guy I met walking down the street heard I was English and told me, although he wasn't meant to say such things anymore, that when the British ran things, there was no corruption, schools were open to all, hospitals functioning and even the traffic lights worked.

The company driver took me back to the airport. Seeing that the traffic was building up in our direction, he drove through the central reservation of what once separated a three lane way highway, and then proceeded to drive the wrong way against the oncoming traffic, whilst I closed my eyes and prayed. They do it all the time he said and there was nothing to worry about, really.

I finally got to the relative sanctuary of the airport. After managing to avoid bribing anyone for anything all week, I got caught by the airport security officials. The very nice smiling lady asked what had set the metal alarm off (my pen) and then asked for it as a gift, whilst holding onto her handgun with one hand and my laptop bag with the other. Her colleague, or accomplice, who was about seven feet tall and holding a machine gun, also asked for a gift. As my matching pen and pencil set no longer matched, I gave him the other piece. Still, a pretty cheap price all things considered.

The whole point of this particular African trip was to review our Subsidiary accounts. I'd spent a day or more reviewing documents, getting increasingly frustrated at the lack of being able to tie things up. I asked our local Financial Controller (FC) what was I missing and was told that we had two sets of books; the real ones for internal reporting and a second official set against which we paid local taxes. Having looked through both sets, we would have ended up paying less tax if we only submitted the correct accounts in the first place. It was pointed out that nobody would believe they were real and we'd still have to "negotiate" with the local authorities anyway. My international auditing experience wasn't going so well.

The French like the French

A few trips to the USA followed, to Dallas and Houston. My French counter parts were allowed to travel on company time, so they flew in on Monday. For some reason, I was required to fly in ready for Monday, which meant a Sunday flight.

Occasional European Financial Controller meetings were held in Paris. In one such meeting, I surveyed the room noting that every other FC, from dozens of countries and projects, was French. The pay was good, the travel fun, but a gradual culture change towards a French owned company not so much. Our MD was "retired", thanked and replaced with a new French MD. His English not so strong, but still better than my French, he set about demonstrating his authority. One evening he kept me working with him on a budget presentation, not that I contributed much, until mid-night when he looked at me, smiled and said "you are released".

With my second son having recently been born, it was time for a re-assessment. I found myself leaving the house before he woke, and arriving home after bedtime. At week-ends, he struggled to recognise me. Family was more important than career, I resigned.

Work out what your own value system is

Connections & coincidences make the world work

My next job was with Roche, a properly big role and one my FTSE100 friend said, again, I'd never get. He was, this time, even more confident that I'd fail to get an interview, much less get the job. He was of course possibly even more right this time!

I took this, quite accurate and correct advice, as a personal challenge and inspiration. It certainly meant that I was at last aiming for a role significantly more senior and out of my comfort zone. This is the place, after all, where all personal growth takes place.

The Swiss FD seemed to have one real concern which was about how to bring back under Finance control all the de-centralised purchasing. I at least had an answer to that question, even if my PowerPoint presentation was somewhat lacking! Actually, it was objectively awful. However, I had spent my years at Prudential, amongst other tasks, bringing remote purchasing into a central environment, for all our multiple acquisitions. This, for me, was an easy question to answer, one which obviously other candidates had failed to make an impression on.

I later found out he was a very keen tennis player and my CV did mention having played at Wimbledon…

The corporate culture was interesting, inasmuch as the business ethics were scrupulous but the language poor! This was the complete reverse of the Oil Co, where phrases involving "end" and "means" spring to mind, but swearing in the office would see you sent home. Swearing and generally living life to full abounded here. It was fun. This was the first company environment I'd discovered where people genuinely enjoyed coming to work. That they happened to be the third largest Pharma Company in the world, employed Nobel Prize winning scientists and made stack loads of money also helped.

So what does make for success?

Although Roche were ruthless in their pursuit of excellence, dominance and growth they had some seriously clever ways of thinking. They took the view that the first mistakes you made were probably their fault for not training or supporting you; this encouraged risk taking and, consequently, success. Repeated failure wasn't a long term option though.

They also recognised the season they were in and staffed and managed accordingly. During a season of high growth expectations we had a sales orientated Managing Director. Understanding that sales cannot be indefinitely sustained, they then brought in an administrative Managing Director to consolidate that growth. It was all very deliberate and it worked.

They invested in staff training, properly and at substantial cost. I spent an entire day learning how to juggle and another a few months later on how to break a thick wooden board with a karate punch. This patently made me a better Financial Controller.

They also invested in a ten day management training programme for potential senior managers, they were serious about their people.

One impactful staff training session highlighted the qualities that made for a successful team. It goes like this; imagine you are rewarded for all your success with a one year all-inclusive Caribbean holiday, on full pay. The only caveat is that you need to recruit your temporary replacement, and you will fly back, at your own cost, to solve whatever problems they cannot fix. Now come up with a list of all the qualities you look for in your temporary replacement. Simple. What followed in our staff session, with about fifty people in attendance, was a list of around thirty qualities. The really interesting bit is that less than five had anything to do with ability and all the others were character related.

Roche assumed that everyone, broadly, could do the job they applied for, what they were looking for was character.

Project roles are exciting (if you are an Accountant reading this)

Financial Controller - Marketing (Near Patient Testing Division) was the role I applied for, and was offered, despite my crap PowerPoint presentation. I turned up on the first day with a tie and was met by Chris, wearing red braces and no tie. "You're in marketing now sonny, you can lose the tie". Oh how I enjoyed this. There was an entire and completely separate Finance Department whose role it was to process orders, sales invoices, purchases, post payroll journals, manage stock takes, deal with auditors, reconcile balance sheet control accounts and work late. And I didn't work in it for once. I reviewed marketing spend and advertising programme costs and assessed impact. I looked at parallel imports and generally looked at data in a wider sense, and what that told us about how we could do things better and consequently make more money. I enjoyed going to work. They even kicked you out the office before six, saying "tired staff aren't any good"!

Roche acquired a small company based up in the Midlands. It complemented the product offering and had its own distribution outlets. The FD felt that it needed understanding, before we could successfully bring it in-house. Being one of two project accountants, and I guess having successfully worked on the Divisional projects, as I had, I was ideally placed. So started a monthly cycle of trips, hotel stays and understanding subsidiary accounting. Being a small company, it was relatively straightforward to get on top of. But their own accountant resigning meant a few more trips and a few more nights away than I wanted. The accounting was eventually brought in house, the company absorbed and the task completed. It's not often in accounting that you get to see an entire job through to a conclusion in this manner, it felt good.

The FD was really getting stuck in by now. Roche were relentless in driving up sales, managing down costs, doing things better and more efficiently. Maybe somewhat surprisingly, for such a large company, purchasing was done by anyone, from anywhere, it was utterly decentralised. This was an opportunity for some serious efficiencies.

The assertions I had made at interview were now being called in. I was to create a Purchasing dept., recruit the staff and over the next few months pull back all the company purchasing activities. This too was a straightforward assignment. Even in large companies, it's the small activities that often count. We proved efficiencies could be made and then delivered them. Duplication eliminated, economies of scale achieved, standardised Service Level Agreements (SLAs) created. Again, a project that had a start, middle and outcome.

Some call it a crisis and buy a Harley

My "mid-life assessment" came at the age of thirty five. I had a pay rise, decent performance bonus, pension and the expense account and even the opportunity to apply for an International Swiss promotional path. Oh that was so tempting!

It dawned on me that I had achieved the, in hindsight rather low, career objectives I'd made some fifteen years ago. My thoughts as a nineteen year old were something along the lines of "if I ever get to earn £50,000 a year I'll have made it". I had. What I had to look forward to now was another twenty five years of the same. It didn't appeal.

What surprised me most was that even though Roche had invested in me, they fully supported my non-career choice. They threw a leaving party and said lots of nice things. The FD awarded me a performance bonus despite my mid-year departure and technical illegibility. In his view I'd contributed to their success that year and was therefore entitled to share the rewards. I remain very impressed with Roche.

Roche has very low staff turnover, Roche is successful

Plans are what you can achieve, set your Dreams much higher

I'd looked long and hard, during my "mid-life assessment" for a role where I could combine accounting with the family in a development context. A few Voluntary Service Overseas (VSO) type enquiries were met with them basically saying "please, you come, but leave the family behind". Eventually, through a friend of a friend, we met with a mentor for several inter-denominational, faith based, and international projects. Again, networking had produced connections that would be instrumental in changing the course of our lives.

It's been pointed out to me several times that I must be a great networker and how hard do I have to work to manage that, and pay attention to it. This makes it sound like a tool, or a trick. Not at all. If I am a good networker, it is by accident. All that I do, as I meet people, is take a genuine interest in them and their story. I like people. I'm not interested in them for my own potential future benefit. I've learned to disconnect or de-couple service and reward. What I mean by this is that helping others, taking an interest in them and valuing them, is its own reward. Completely by accident, we've found, repeatedly over time, that others deal with us in the same manner. It is empowering. Love others, basically. It could also be seen as a type of "karma", if that helps!

The question he posed to us was simple; if we had a map of the world in front of us, where were we drawn to? I confess to being taken aback, we were just a minute into a conversation about who we were, getting ready to share our journey and he asked this brilliant question. Mrs M and I looked at each other and both said the Caribbean. It was a surprise as it was not hitherto a question we had in fact asked, even to each other. Having an identical answer was a revelation. I can hear the groans you're emitting even now, of course the Caribbean, who wouldn't?

I'd been made redundant from Prudential back in 1991 and bought essentially the most exotic honeymoon £5,000 would buy. Two weeks in St Lucia in a five star hotel with just about every extra possible. It was a truly amazing experience and I know we have been privileged to have had it. However, both my wife and I, even back then, were explorers and we loved dipping out of the tourist melee and wandering into whatever the local community was. One Sunday we decided to walk to the nearest church, had an enjoyable time being the only white faces in the room and were met with nothing but loving kindness, including Sunday lunch with a random stranger we met walking out the door. Other times we saw the poverty people had to contend with. We were told the history of how the World Trade organisation (WTO) was used by the USA to bankrupt the local banana economy. The story is that the UK used to purchase all the entire crop, supporting an entire nation's economy. The WTO were used to render this arrangement counter-competitive and opened the door to a small number of Florida famers discounting the market and taking their market. The visit left a distinct mark in my memory. That day, in that office, the question took me right back to that country and region, and I found myself asking whether I could in fact make a difference there.

Ally for her part had supported a young Dominican Republic boy for fifteen years through Tear-Fund's child sponsorship programme, and this drove her off-the-cuff response.

The more impressive thing was that he knew of several projects in Jamaica, was visiting there in two weeks and so he asked whether we would like to go and take a look?

Favour is a strange looking beast. To some it's money, for us it was people saying "yes" to questions where the answer would normally be "no". We'd just come back from a family skiing holiday in the south of France. Working for a multi-billion pharmaceutical company is generally well paid after all. I was back in work a day and went in to ask whether I could take the following week off, to which the answer was "yes". Having splashed the cash on the holiday, I didn't have a spare £1,000 to get a flight, but fortunately several business flights with the American Music Company meant sufficient air miles for a free flight, and they had one going the next week I could take. After months of frustration and nothing, all of a sudden, I was on a plane to Jamaica.

That visit introduced me to a couple of projects, one of which I felt would fit my skills, but more importantly, provide Ally and our two boys a relatively safer and more welcoming environment.

We'd discussed how and when we'd tell the boys we were moving across the ocean to Jamaica. Looking through the TV listings, these were the days before the Sky TV planner, I noticed that "Cool Runnings" happened to be on that afternoon. I love coincidences. It's easy to manipulate young children and exert pressure as parents, so we were keen to make sure that the boys were genuinely excited about the move. The film helped!

I'd decided that Montego Bay was the right project and the right place. Flying Ally and the boys out a couple of months later I hoped they'd feel the same too. I knew enough that if they hated it, I'd also come to hate it if I forced it upon them.

They approved, well the missus approved and that's what really counted.

Generosity blows people away, and once you embrace it, is really fun

We rented out our house, and gave away nearly everything of value that we owned. We took the stance that seeing as we would be volunteers and therefore reliant upon friends and family for their generosity, we should at least demonstrate that in our own lives first.

This lead to a great and fun adventure; being totally open handed and generous with your possessions. We didn't realise how counter cultural this was at the time.

Give away the best of what you have and dump the crap. We hadn't thought of doing that in any special way, except after someone gave us second-hand socks to allegedly help us out. After that we resolved only ever to give things away that would genuinely be a blessing to those on the receiving end!

It sounds easy looking back on it now, but of course it was a journey. We hadn't quite appreciated that our materialistic British society valued "having" so much. It's also a revelation to begin to see how often gifts are given with strings attached. The fun for us was then doing things completely opposite to this and watching people's reactions. Some of our friends embraced the "take what you like" option quite enthusiastically once they saw we meant it. Others just couldn't get over their own issues with being given things for free and with no preconditions.

We eventually worked our way up to giving cars and motorbikes away. Subsequently, accidentally, coincidentally even, wherever we've travelled we have found that cars and bikes become available to us, and almost always for free.

It's got to the point that I no longer concern myself with transport at destinations. Just last week for example, in Switzerland, a friend threw their bike keys at me and said to enjoy the week-end on it.

Living in the Caribbean, tough gig?

If you look at my CV you'll see the grand job title of Business and Operations Manager for a College. Let's just say that the organisation didn't quite live up to the promotional material and personal endorsements by those I met on the initial two visits. I took a week to settle Ally and the boys in, and got them into the school we wanted. Jordan was by now six and Joel would soon be four.

We flew out September 13th 2001, just two days after the events of 9/11. The whole world was turned upside down and we were shocked to be confronted by how many people were gloating that the US had got what was coming to them. I was horrified. Being British, one is sheltered from the tangible affect the US's foreign policy, whether obvious or covert, has on other nations. It appeared as though people grudgingly respected power, but once a weakness was exposed, felt it was open season on releasing pent up aggression towards them.

The tourist economy in Jamaica took a substantial and immediate hit, as did the foreign visitors to the college campus, which in previous months was the only thing keeping it solvent. It took a little while to fully understand this of course, as I grappled with an organisation nose-diving into insolvency.

Pirates of the Caribbean is a thing

We had shipped out boxes and suitcases and toys (including my windsurf board) a couple of months earlier; basically our life in a space the size of a transit van. Unfortunately, the previous container ship to ours had been hijacked by pirates! They were temporarily not stopping into Montego Bay as it was less secure than Kingston. Those people from Kingston talked about Montego Bay, or Mobay, as being some out-in-the-sticks place. Having deliberately packed light for the journey, so as to have hands free with our two young sons, we were now living out of a suitcase each for the next few weeks, until it all got delivered.

The real adventure begins

We'd been promised a detached house on top of the hill. However, when we arrived, they'd changed their minds and given it to another family from Canada, and assigned us an "apartment" on the end of the girls' dormitory wing. The apartment was sort of separate, but felt very close to everyone else, not truly private. We were gracious and accepted it though, partly because we now had a simply stunning view right out across Montego Bay and the port.

We'd been there less than a week, and just got the boys into school and started making the apartment a home. We encountered our first hurricane. Announcements over the radio warned us of the impending winds and rain, and we were advised to take everything down off shelves, apply gorilla or duct tape across all the glass windows and settle in under the kitchen table. We then had to pretend to the boys that this was entirely normal and there was absolutely nothing to worry about!

My first day in the office was a shock; wearing smart trousers and shirt and sweating very badly from the hundred yard walk up the hill. We didn't have a/c in the room but did have a ceiling fan. Any time after 6am, as soon as you stepped out from under the fan the sweat started running quite freely. It took a few months to adjust, but after a while we ended up "feeling" the colder nights and took to wearing pyjamas and having a duvet and I even went to work with a jacket on.

I was given the reports from the exiting Business Manager and handed the passwords to the accounting system. I then spent a very confusing few hours pondering how the College was still in existence, as they had nowhere near enough cash coming in to cover the basic operating costs. Not even close. I gently asked the manager about this, who then informed me that "you people are all the same and you don't know nuttin"! The College lasted a few short weeks and finally went bankrupt and operations stopped. Visiting tourists had previously brought in precious currency, but 9/11 had stopped all tourist traffic in its tracks. The college had, even then, been propped up by a series of occasional "donations" over several months, but even the latest donation wasn't enough to pay the bills. Having been originally set up, funded and overseen by a US based world-wide organisation, they went to them for yet more bailouts which were being refused.

Now things got really interesting. The local Director left, without saying much to anyone, except to load up a bus with all their things and leave late one night.

We had arrived a few weeks prior at the same time as a Canadian family, the father of which had come to teach in the College and the mother would be home-schooling their children. Art & Deb had both given up decent and secure roles as a Church Pastors, bringing their children out of a safe Canadian environment to the apparent wild-west which was Montego Bay. Art and I took on the management, which was basically attempting to oversee an orderly closure, cessation of activities and moth-balling of the site. It was a former hotel, with accommodation for over three hundred, swimming pool, conference facilities, radio station and staff accommodation. It even had its own chicken farm. Art never got to teach a single lesson.

We'd also connected with an American family, from Virginia, who were running a significant residential charity for deaf children. These would become some of our very best and dearest friends. They were also a lifeline in our new and challenging circumstances.

Having run out of cash and still having our two families on base, plus several staff and students that had yet to leave, things had to get a little creative. One student managed to convince a local Chinese restaurant that we could fulfil his weekend chicken order. So we slaughtered twenty or so chickens and filled a black sack with the bodies and drove it downtown and into the back of this "quality" establishment, and walked out with a wad of cash. That was then taken down the market in the morning and swapped for food for a week! On another occasion I swapped chickens for petrol for the pickup at the local garage.

All was going well using our chicken currency (an average chicken weights 4lb with a street value of $1/lb) until the local community heard we'd been shut down. They promptly invaded overnight, took the remaining four hundred chickens plus equipment, fencing, a generator, tools from the sheds and whatever else they could find. We didn't hear a thing.

I talked with the senior management in the US who came to visit and to finally see what was really happening. We, having given away all our possessions and rented out our home in the UK, were committed to seeing this season through. They were grateful I think that someone sensible was prepared to volunteer to manage everything for them. They didn't seem very much at ease in this environment at all! They then sent money to settle the various creditors, and I wrote the books up drawing it all to a close. These included several years of unpaid taxes and social security that they hadn't acted upon yet. I found this out only once I started meeting with the local tax authorities and started to unravel the history, or lack of it.

The Jamaican students did all leave, once we no longer had money for food and started shutting down and securing the dormitories.

We managed to get enough money to keep the security guys on for a while and the maintenance manager, as he was the only one who could keep the water pipes from pissing away the $ (the plumbers had installed all the plastic water pipes above ground and the sunlight UV was destroying it continually, and quickly). One month we spent $2,000 on water as it leaked out all over the grounds.

I decided that, apart from everything else, the site ought to be brought back into order ready for whoever the new owners might be. The local Jamaican "landscaping" and propensity towards doing the least–hard thing, had meant that they'd used the fish pond to hide all their trash rather than take it to the city dump! So, this qualified and relatively senior accountant would routinely spend his afternoons picking up metalwork, and years of rubbish from around the site and take it to the dump. We met families who lived amongst the rubbish and got to see a side of Jamaican poverty we'd not yet come across.

The action shot that is my "bio" on the back cover was on a typical day during this season.

The Canadian family temporarily adopted two teenage twin boys who were Wards of Court of the College's now absent Director. These boys had previously slept on their Kingston bedroom floor at night to avoid the bullets coming through their windows. We adopted a third, together with one staff member, who despite being older than my wife, still calls her "mom"! Troy was a challenge, although he could be very funny and charming, he had some obvious authority issues! He'd witnessed his best friend being hacked to death in Kingston and had no family. Andrea was a joy and still sends us Mother and Father Day greetings after all these years.

The Haitian students were the hardest to encourage to leave, understandably, however the College was technically responsible (through their visa permissions) for them being there. The only way to get them to leave was to take them to the airport. We even paid for one of the flights to make sure they left!

Organisations have informal communication, countries too

So much to learn. When we arrived, we had been assured that getting a work permit would be straightforward, "no problem mon". At my first interaction with the local authorities, I was told to go home, to the UK, and apply for a visa from there. Back at the College they said to ignore this and we'd be going up to Kingston in a couple of weeks and it would all be sorted. I then felt that every Police officer was to be avoided and that somehow I was there under false pretences. Well, I still don't know what the real true situation was, but it worked out eventually.

The work permit came through a couple of days before the College went bankrupt and closed.

Work became a mix of managing the security, grounds and maintenance staff and attempting to bring some kind of order to the eleven acre twenty building complex. I learnt how to clean the swimming pool and Art and I took on the pool maintenance between us – a not insignificant task and one my accounting training hadn't really mentioned at any stage. I've checked, it's not in any of the text books I studied. The green algae of the 2016 Rio Olympics was a frequent early occurrence for us until we learned the intricacies and tell-tale signs ourselves.

One learns that things are easier as a local. Despite my obviously British accent, a few well-placed local patois phrases in a half-decent accent made a real difference to how I was treated. We also obtained a local driving licence which "proved" this beyond doubt when obtaining discounts. There was a dual price system in place for attractions, one for locals and one for foreigners.

We were, however, stopped on several occasions and asked how come we'd been given permission to adopt Jamaican children. Sometimes these questions were quite aggressive. Jamaicans are blunt. They will say all sorts of things to your face if they think you're doing anything wrong, including frequent suggestions on how you can be better parents! Our boys were so acclimatised to the local culture, attending Primary School day in day out for two years will do that for you, that everyone thought they were Jamaican. Despite our protestations, I don't think we ever convinced anyone that we hadn't somehow bribed our way into adopting two Jamaican orphans. My eldest, Jordan, will still occasionally whistle through his teeth if he's annoyed. Joel was too young and now no longer talks like a Jamaican!

I must have looked local to some though. A British friend, Jamaican by birth but who had lived most of his life in the UK, was in Montego Bay teaching at the boy's school. He'd been here only a short while and we were walking down the street. A "relaxed" Rasta, sitting by the roadside called out "hey whitey" to us and my friend looked at me and smiled. "No mon, I'm talking to the Londoner" and pointed at my black Jamaican friend. It was a bizarre and proud moment, somehow I "looked" local. I felt as though I fitted and belonged. "Whitey" wasn't as happy though!

One of the parents of the friends the boys had made owned the water sports concession at a seriously up market hotel, Round Hill Resort. Half joking one day he told us that "you white people all look the same to me". He was white himself, a Jamaican of many generations, and Jamaicans, we discovered, think they're all simply different shades of brown.

The boys enjoyed Montego Bay. One friend of ours was seeing an Air Traffic Controller, and one night we stopped by to visit with him, at work. The boys still recall how they got to play with all the airport and runway lights, during a gap in flight activity. I do mean all the lights, on all the runways, on the entire airport, directly from the tower. I'm sure it was all entirely in order for us to be up there. The US government had paid for a radar control system, but the local government hadn't paid for the staff to be trained in how to use it. So, the controllers still had to visualise every flight, in order to track them in to land.

Bumping up the qualifications for my C.V.

Wherever we have found ourselves, we, and now our sons, try to embrace the local culture, place and attractions. It takes discipline and it is a strong conscious decision. Too often, I think, one is so preoccupied with daily life, that what's available around us gets lost a little.

I'd passed a dive-shop and, in chatting to local friends, seen that many of the cruise ships come in and guests pay handsomely to go scuba diving off the local reefs. These are amazing, and water warm and clear.

I happened to bump into a scuba instructor and mentioned I'd be interested in learning to dive. However, being local, and doing voluntary work, couldn't pay tourist prices. We negotiated a seriously reduced price and over the next few months I would take the PADI open water diving course. I'd promise to read the manuals during the week, and then he'd take me out for a couple of dives on the Friday and I'd be tested practically. I do get claustrophobic and am nervous around water, but, scuba diving in Jamaica, I had to master it. The thrill of the dive outweighed fear of dying, basically.

We even had a day introducing the boys to diving; Jordan just old enough to use the scuba assist kit and Joel learning how to snorkel properly.

I'd shipped out my windsurf board, and was trying a new location, off a beach down-town. As I was dragging the kit up the beach, a local gentlemen stopped to help and chat. I would have been a rare sight for sure. He was a self-employed Dive-master and earned his living taking rich tourists out for scuba experiences whenever the cruise ships turned up. As we got chatting about diving, he suggested I could take my diving to the next level and why not try the Advanced PADI? Again, with a "mates-rates" price agreed, I went through the five mandatory advanced dives required for certification.

Now, Jamaicans have a completely different value system towards safety, and I'd acclimatised so much, that we were, in hindsight and looking back from the UK, a little too relaxed when diving.

Let's just say that the "night-dive" ought to have had more to it than just the two of us and a torch. The "deep-dive" involved a descent down a very tall very and extremely narrow coral chimney. This then opened out into a cave, one hundred and twenty feet below, and that cave then exited directly out onto the edge of the Cayman Trench. The danger of deep diving is the intoxicating impact it has on the brain, to the extent that people routinely believe they can breathe under water and remove their apparatus. I resisted this and performed the mandatory mental agility tests as required, but somehow managed to misspell my name! Diving friends back in Eastbourne would later be horrified to learn about my experiences. From the relative safety of a British sofa, they all agreed I'd had a very close shave indeed.

Different cultural business practices for the naïve / uninitiated

Getting work done was a huge learning curve. Straight out of UK Corporate culture, I was used to deadlines, task lists, outcomes, accomplishment, and closure. Queuing at the bank would now frequently take hours, and then at the counter you had to have a working relationship with some of the staff in order to move anything along. There were always problems to be resolved and nothing was ever straightforward. All the utility bills had to be paid in person. More queues, and then problems with paperwork or lost receipts. The power of receipts, and the danger of losing your proof that a bill had been paid, was real. In Sierra Leone a colleague had deposited company funds into an account but forgot the receipt, the counter clerk pocketed the money and because he had no proof, the cash was lost. Electricity routinely got cut off, necessitating a visit to the cash desk down town to try and resolve it, but it might take several visits before you got to see anyone with the authority required to effect a change.

Oh how I missed the UK at those times, when you could pay a bill and simply trust that the person taking the money was part of a well-oiled and integrity based system to ensure everything was duly processed. Many years later a highly placed lawyer friend confided that our entire British legal system was once corrupt, and that court fees were brought in simply to ensure that everyone effectively paid the same "bribe" and in that way helped judges to dispense justice freely.

Time is indeed relative

It took several weeks. I began to realise that I could still have my task-list, for indeed there were a dozen things needing doing every day, but it became a holistic circle of events and people and meetings and interactions, some of which may well result in movement but many of which were simply part of the general fabric of the day. If that sounds loose and vague and long winded, it was. I relaxed. I took to stopping in at the Rite Café for an eleven o'clock Jamaican coffee, with sweetened condensed milk as is the custom, and my day would feel much better. Everything was now in order and balanced. Generally, things did eventually happen, and some of the things on the list would get crossed off and new things would appear, but I was no longer stressed, I was part of a new way of working. And, it all functioned, life carried on. Time was less important, I no longer wore a watch, people and places became of more value.

In the early days I'd turn up for meetings with the college director and the senior management team. He'd often take a call and we'd have to sit there and wait for him as he smiled and generally wasted my important time. I would get, internally at least, extremely cross. It was wasting my time, disrespectful, somethings Jamaicans are really bothered about, and obviously a power play to establish the true pecking order. After all, in my experience this was true, my new French boss at the Oil Company would sometimes do similar things, and he wasn't even subtle about what he was doing. I was even sure that it was some sort of British / historical / Judeo-Christian truth that we should honour each other's time. Nothing changed, and nobody else seemed remotely bothered. With more and more such events taking place over the coming weeks, it gradually dawned on me that this was no power play; rather that "time" itself was a less important concept here. The thing of value was that we were together, time was irrelevant. I then realised that punctuality, as drilled in to me by my own father, who would prefer to be an hour early than a minute late, was entirely my own cultural artefact. I was appalled at myself for my frequent angry judgements aimed at people who would keep me waiting at meetings.

The final nail in this particular coffin came at a wedding event we were invited to. A famous local band, who we had met somehow, were performing, and the wedding started at 3pm. They arrived at 6pm, nobody was even the slightest bit bothered. It had taken them three hours to drive from Kingston, they had started the event "on time" inasmuch as they'd left home at 3pm. I think that was the night I took my watch off.

I try not to wear a watch even today, just to try and re-connect myself to a different way of doing things. There are multiple ways of telling time in our culture anyway.

Our money gets rinsed

We were desperate for our own wheels. So far we'd relied on jumping into the base pickup truck as and when it was running errands around town. Not at all reliable and not what a middle-aged businessman with a family was used to, nor his wife.

We'd been fed a diet of horror stories by our friends about not getting into taxis, about being targeted, not for being white, but for appearing wealthy, which whiter people generally were. Andrea had been threatened in a taxi recently with a jar of sulphuric acid. We were told to take off all gold jewellery, as if the ring didn't come right off, they'd chop your finger off to save time. Many Jamaican men carried a machete in their cars, alongside the seat, so they could leap out the car, machete in hand, if they needed to. We went to a local tourist shop and bought silver rings and took our gold wedding rings off and hid them away. Art & Deb, being ordained Ministers, blessed them, which gave a legitimacy to the whole process.

The helpful driver employed by the college suggested a friend of his who could help us import a car, which is what most people do, apparently, as Jamaican second-hand cars were so badly bashed up. The roads were truly awful. There were no used car lots in Montego Bay. We gave him our three thousand pounds and waited for the next ship from Japan to arrive. Japanese cars are routinely dumped when they are three years old, as the MOT system there is so punitive it's cheaper generally to buy new again. They drive on the "right" side of the road and so Jamaica imports them, nearly or as-new and everyone is happy. Our boat didn't arrive. Weekly visits to the import office were, I have to say impressively, rebuffed with genuine sounding reason after genuine sounding reason, week after week after week. They had this down to an art form.

As the college winding down process was drawing to a conclusion, I turned to other opportunities and local charities. Having sound accounting and commercial experience means a huge amount compared to the training, experience and education levels available locally. I was invited to undertake a financial performance analysis for "Teamwork" a community based primary and secondary school plus agricultural centre outside of town. It had been set up by Menzie Oban who had despaired of seeing children on the streets, not attending school and being failed by society. He single-handedly built everything from scratch and established an amazing school site. He was famous locally for approaching businesses, both honest and less than honest, and coming away with donations and help. His totally unique personality seemed to bash through all sorts of social norms. The business side of this amazing project though was not clear and not healthy and I spent several days there looking into different aspects of what they did and how they did it, to report back to their Trustee Board.

At their next General Meeting I sat beside one of the Trustees, who happened to be a bailiff. In sharing the story of my car he said he'd make a call on my behalf and see if he could help. Apparently my money was being used to "rinse" cars through the system, it was essentially seed capital they hadn't needed to find, that would import a car, which would then be sold, then used again, hence rinse cycle, to obtain the next one. I had my money the next week. It seemed as though my selfless act of service for teamwork had yielded an unexpected benefit.

Water someone else's garden and trust that someone will water yours

As the college was winding down, the creditors started to turn up. One guy arrived for a debt, I can scarcely remember the details of which, but he strangely described himself as a "big-man". This was a peculiar sounding phrase. I checked this out with some friends and they casually said this meant he had a gun, was likely a bailiff, and had basically warned me that he would be using his gun if he didn't get what he wanted. That helpfully shaped my focus for the next week! Somehow I managed to get his money together and he was perfectly nice when we next met. It sounds very casual to say this now, but, I had spent a very anxious week indeed scrambling around to get money together to settle this particular debt!

I then understood that my trustee friend, being a bailiff, was also likely a "big-man" himself and I was grateful for his own intervention on my behalf!

In helping the college resolve all its complex and plentiful winding up issues, the US Owners said that we could have the Toyota 4WD. I loved this vehicle, basically the Top-Gear team's favourite vehicle. It was big, twin cabbed, four wheel drive, and red and big and strong and reliable. However, it didn't quite sit right with us. We felt sorry for the potential new owners who would arrive to run this large and complex site but have no vehicle, which we knew to be hard to come by. On the way home from one downtown trip, we resolved to hand them the pick-up.

Meanwhile, the US side had likewise felt sorry for us, the Meggs family, who had been offered a two year contract which included at least free food at the college canteen. Without us knowing they were thinking through this, they had calculated a financial sum they thought matched to the value of our lost free meals and had sent an email with this, a promise of several thousand US dollars! The email arrived around the time we were driving up the hill to hand the pick-up over.

With that money, we eventually did buy our own car, through a friend, an amazing ex-military or ex-consular Toyota Crown. It had blacked out windows, and special extras such as a fridge in the back seat to keep beer or chocolate cold! It drew a lot of attention. I became very local and installed a kick-arse sound system that you could feel in your stomach before you could hear. Reggae sound was ever present at night where we lived, and so music and noise simply became a part of our own new culture.

I discovered that the College had not properly paid its taxes, despite the Director having told the US team that everything was all clear. The computer records at the tax office were not at all clear, and would have likely remained undiscovered for a long time, possibly. My attempt at an orderly closure did however bring this right into the light! Much was owed and I managed to negotiate a payment plan that was affordable to the US side. It cost them, but it was the right thing to do. Not paying taxes is part of the reason the local infrastructure didn't work.

Mrs M and I were invited to be interviewed for a local TV station. Don't know how that happened or what people thought of it, but we had our fifteen minutes of fame.

Mrs M volunteered at the boy's primary school. Well, for the first year, when we had no transport, she'd travel in the school bus to ensure Joel got to school. He was after all only just four years old and it was an hour plus journey through the melee of downtown Montego Bay just to get to school. So she stayed, and volunteered in the school office. Humbling for her, as a qualified and extremely able primary school teacher herself. However, she was there as a Mum, Joel her only concern. Jordan, at six years old, seemed so much older we scarcely worried. He had a punch up on his first day of school and after that he fell in with a likely bunch of lads and had a great time. He was frequently punished for talking, as they all were. He also learned that authority in Jamaica is different. You don't look up, you look down. They both learned how to communicate. Most educated Jamaicans can speak the middle class English we would all know, and they can also all turn on the street style when needed, always met with shouts of approval if done in a public setting.

We had to un-learn that behaviour when back in the UK, where not looking in the eyes of authority is deemed rude, not submissive.

When is colour learned?

Jordan and Joel had been at the school for a few days. As I arrived in the borrowed pick-up to collect them, Jordan came running out with a coloured-in picture of him and his class mates. "Look" he said, "you can tell which one I am can't you?" Of course I could, I thought, you're the only white boy in the class for a start, matey. "I'm the one with freckles on my nose". Ouch and ouch again. Apparently, so the boys would later say when asked, they and their classmates see everyone as shades of brown. When and how did I perceive colour as the most immediate differentiating factor when meeting people?

I installed an accounting package for the school, as you do. They all assumed because I was an accountant that this would be a piece of cake. This was the first time when I'd assumed total control of such a project and I did take it seriously. However, the software and accounting world had undergone much progress since the days of DOS based systems and tape reels. QuickBooks was easy to load and everything balanced and the double entry worked. It took a few days to load up the opening balances, but I had now successfully installed an entire accounting system for a client.

The church we attended was a new one and they were keen to offer practical humanitarian assistance in the local community. I set up their accounting systems also.

The friend said she might be able to help with finding new accommodation as we'd had to move out of the college when the new owners took up possession. Having lost our free home, we were now beginning to struggle with how to survive on £700 total family income a month.

A couple in the church said they'd a spare house on their estate that we could use. Oh wow! This family were in fact the descendants of the first British ships to arrive in Jamaica back in the 1600s and had been there for multiple generations. Our cottage was the cook's and servant's quarters for the first and original Great-house. It was just off the long private drive to the estate, on a large sugar cane plantation, overlooking the waters of Montego Bay in the distance. They were kind and generous and sacrificed guaranteed rental income in order to help us. I remain grateful to them always. The great house is called Bellefield and has featured on TV documentaries and is included in the list of top ten attractions for Montego Bay.

The servant's quarters were not. It was also a shed on stilts, infested with insects and all sorts of poisonous wildlife, one of which nearly killed my eldest.

The MV Logos ii came to town. This ship is described as the world's largest floating library and is also used for emergency and medical relief when disasters strike in the region. Someone had heard that we had empty a number of empty properties on the campus complex, a laughable understatement of course, and we might be able to host their advance team. So we housed several of them for the weeks leading up to the visit, as they prepared the way and set everything up for the ship coming to town. We were invited to see round and were further asked to help their senior staff when they arrived. The First Mate was a keen scuba diver and I sacrificially arranged a day's diving with him whilst in port. It was interesting to take a tour of the anti-piracy gear, basically deck mounted water cannons, as they discussed what course they would chart to leave Montego Bay, so as to avoid the pirates. Pirates are real remember.

As the new owners took up residency, I cleared out an old concrete basement storage room, and set about filing and recording all the paperwork from the old college. It was not glamorous, I had rats for company, a dusty desk in a dimly lit store-room and an old, barely functioning, computer. It was there to provide "receipts" in case they were ever needed in the future.

The US based college owners recognised that they'd failed in their charitable endeavours and wanted to finish honourably, and commendably so. They had personal connections to another large charity and so gifted the entire complex to them, no strings attached.

Youth with a Mission (YWAM) successfully works with young people all around the world. They have around twenty thousand volunteers in over two hundred countries in a thousand plus locations. Unpaid volunteers need no salary, and the organisation has no debt. They made a gift of this multi-million dollar site and we were able to be involved with the ceremonial handing over of the keys.

For all the financial costs they'd incurred, I would have for sure thought they'd want to sell and keep the money to fund their other projects. They had failed and they wanted to pass on their asset to an organisation they trusted to succeed. I learned a great lesson in generosity and integrity that day.

We got to see another small local charity and spent some of week-ends hanging out. They lived right on the sea, and so it seemed only right that I joined in and learned how to fish using a spear-gun. I was told that you try to chase the fish, who swim off way quicker than you can. However, they always stop and turn around to see if the danger has gone away, and that's when you shoot the spear at them. I assumed they were pulling my leg, until I saw this behaviour for myself. I could now bring home lunch! The same day I was learning to spear fish, their children were showing my boys how to look down the storm drains to see how many crocodiles were there. Jamaica.

I received a call from someone setting up a brand new youth training programme in down-town Montego Bay, called Youth Enhancement Services (YES). I arrived thinking I was there to discuss QuickBooks or Sage or whatever, and that they wanted me to manage their finances. However, the principal wanted to talk about whether I might be interested, and available, to help deliver a class for her. As I sort of agreed, this then became two classes, neither class had notes or a curriculum and both would require assessment and examinations at the end of the year... I'd been quite successfully played! This did however become one of my more successful and enjoyable accomplishments. I was even invited to their ten year anniversary where they paid respect to those who had laid the foundations for this now nationally renowned and award-winning enterprise. It was a very tangible way of decanting my accounting and business experience. My own training in "personal financial management" and "time management" was now being delivered in a culturally relevant way to an entirely different audience.

Middle class sports still open doors

I took my tennis rackets with me, in case there would be any opportunity to play. A friend Ally had made heard her make some passing reference to me having played tennis at Wimbledon.

Tennis with "Columbian Jimmy"

And so started my most enjoyable tennis season ever. Simon and Nicky lived in a great gated community neat Montego Bay Yacht Club, with its own pool but more importantly, floodlit tennis court. We were generously invited in and made very welcome. Every Tuesday evening several of his friends would gather for a doubles game. Simon was a project Director for Sandals ®, looking after refurbishments and new acquisitions. Another couple were Indian businessmen who had the airport concessions for high end jewellery and gifts. They were not poor and had houses in the most exclusive beachfront district in town. Then there was Jimmy. His job was a little vague, and it took many weeks and the occasional clue to really figure him out. He would be seen in a white stretch limo, and was frequently away on shopping trips to Panama. The final hint was when I bumped into someone in town who had heard I was playing tennis with "Columbian Jimmy"! Jamaicans trash talk. They are blunt in describing your failings. So, for two hours every Tuesday night, we'd get together and simply be competitive tennis players with all the trash talking and bravado and winning that such activities require. Fun, once I'd accepted that for those two hours, we were all *only* tennis players!

My wife is a more spiritual person than I, and had invited Jimmy's girlfriend to a small Alpha Course ® whilst we were playing tennis. When it came time to dedicate their baby, they chose our little church. It was a strange sight to behold half a dozen stretch limousines in the church grounds that particular Sunday morning for sure.

Windsurfing with sharks

There was nobody wind-surfing, save for the occasional German on holiday in an all-inclusive, and therefore exclusive and expensive, resort. Down the road from us was the Reading Reef Hotel, which was on the beach of a secluded but substantial bay. At the mouth was a reef, and this, in my mind, meant it would be safe if I got into trouble with the prevailing seaward wind, as I'd be able to stop there. I had by now fully engaged with a different sense of what is safe and not, Jamaican style.

So, on a Saturday morning I'd wander with the family down to the Hotel, which never had any guests in all the time we visited. Ally would sit with a coke by the pool whilst the boys played in the sand and I'd set out for a few blasts out across the bay. I rarely fell in. This was fortunate, later finding out this is where sharks come to breed. Human and animal Mums tend not to be kind and gentle when they have vulnerable young! I wasn't even aware of that unique danger.

Seasons, cultures and dreams

Our time was drawing to a close. Our income was unsustainable, and the various short term projects we were involved with were all drawing to a close. Life was more expensive than our income. For a season, and actually with quiet ease, Mrs M and I resolved to eat alternate days only. I looked slim and muscular, so that was good, but Mrs M didn't need to lose any more weight!

It was either go down the main-stream job route again, which would have really only meant finding work for a hotel, or return back to the UK. I was sorely tempted to just get a job there!

Having bought our return British Airways (BA) tickets a year earlier, we turned what we thought was an annual visit into a final return home flight. BA had however changed their policy on transporting pets during the year and so we had no choice other than to leave Rex and Coco, our pet guard dogs, in Jamaica. We were close friends with the managers of the Children's Residential deaf Campus and we donated the dogs to them for security. As we visited over the next few weeks we were astonished to see just how much sign language, our up to now our almost unmanageable, Doberman dogs had acquired. Of course the children and staff don't speak and so every interaction is transacted through non-verbal means.

The brutality of Jamaican culture was brought home to us one night as we sat listening to stories with our dear friends Keith and Carole from Virginia. It wasn't the stories about local police coming into their neighbourhood and being stripped naked and told to run off, nor the vapour trails that the bullets left as they whizzed by their front door some evenings. No, it was in fact the story about their Gardener. The Gardener is deaf, as are most of the staff at the school, a residential deaf community for children, the majority of which are otherwise subject to abuse. He was in the office, on the second floor of the building which formed part of the boundary and security wall between them and the local community, where the bullets come from. One day whilst talking to the manager, he noticed a hand appear on the windowsill, without thinking, or even stopping, he whipped out his machete and slashed at the hand, taking off several fingers, which lay there long after their owner picked himself off the ground below and ran off. It was as much the acceptance that this was normal and somehow appropriate that was shocking, not the actual violence and permanent nature of the act itself.

We'd had the incident with Jordan of the "forty-legger", a poisonous millipede, biting him in the middle of the night. Although the car would not start and being unable to get him to medical care, we had a strong sense that he'd be okay with an ice-cube on the bite. Despite hearing of grown men being taken to hospital with paralysed limbs and apocryphal stories that they can kill, we came to a moment of peace and put him back to bed. He woke up with the bite marks still visible but no pain nor paralysis.

I'd had a weird dream, a few days earlier, that evil was coming for Joel. I dismissed it as heat exhaustion, which happens in such climates. Flu doesn't just get people in the cold and damp UK. There had been torrential rain, a tropical storm, just below the hurricane category, and the local sewerage treatment plant had overflowed its contents. Water on the island is naturally filtered through limestone, and undergoes no additional processing before consumption. All well and good, until the sewerage overflows and contaminates the water table. Joel got sick, very badly sick, dysentery sick. Nothing stayed down, and water came squirting out one end immediately we'd given him a drink at the other. He wasn't speaking. This being the day before we were due to fly home, airline friends told us that they would refuse to take us on board if they knew he was ill. BA had changed its flying patterns and no longer served Montego Bay; we'd worked out it was actually quicker, and cheaper and likely safer to charter a private four seater plane than to chance a taxi. We are a family of faith and had no other choice than to pray. We knew we had to get home, it had been such a tough year we needed the break. Ally carried Joel in her arms and I carried the luggage. We landed in the charter Cessna right in front of the gates and somehow were lead through security to the front of the long queue by some mysterious stranger, and invited to board ahead of everyone else. I honestly don't know how or why, but everything just laid itself out for us. Joel was limp as a rag and asleep. As we landed back at Heathrow he started to pick up and was back talking again the next day.

Try and understand your own culture through another's eyes, don't judge theirs until you've lived it

Reverse "culture shock" is a real thing

Our time being adventurous in Jamaica drew to a close. The project we went out to help was by now of course defunct and our financial supporters suggested a period of reflection back home. Ally's Mum was by now in serious medical need, and her Dad needed support in being the main carer. Anyway, we were in the end content to return.

Culture shock is worse on the way back

Being back was a challenge; reverse culture shock, we later learned, was probably as bad as initial culture shock. When you go out somewhere, anywhere unfamiliar really, the well informed, the clever, the wise amongst us, undertake research as to what the new place will be like. Food, temperature, cultural expectations, customs and even some basic language acquisition are all vigorously learnt in eager anticipation of being able to get by with some comfort when we arrive "there".

My father, a long serving Police Officer with a decent stint on Traffic, would remind us that the signs, such as "Drive on the left", as you leave Dover on the A2 heading back into England are not there just for the visitors, they are as much there for the returning Brits. Experience has shown the Police, the Council and the Highways Agency that we don't think about changing habits, newly and consciously acquired, when we return home are safe again. We are so happy to be back that we don't switch off the different way of thinking we've just been using so deliberately.

And so we had come back to the UK full of stories and excitement about what we'd been doing. We assumed everyone would be pleased to see us, and would want to hear about all we'd been doing. We'd assumed that everything would feel familiar again.

We were mostly wrong.

Two years is plenty of time for friends to move on, for the spaces you once filled to have closed over and for new relationships to have taken their place. We are different people too. Our experiences and wider view of the world meant that what was once comfortable could now feel jarring and out of sync. Those we had left behind had naturally been getting on with the business of getting on, and had all, rightly, moved on. They were of course pleased to see us, but mostly we were an interesting and brief aside in their busy day.

We'd not had coaching and were not part of an established charity (NGO) nor had we been sent out by some fancy International Company. Both these types of organisations, we would later learn, take this culture and reverse culture shock very seriously and plan for it appropriately. These organisation's success is built on people, and they've learnt that broken people don't bring success.

Ally and I felt like foreigners again. Language, cultural references, sense of humour, politics, were all somehow slightly different to how we remembered. Some things felt good, but not everything. The boys were unable to re-join their local primary school, despite it being the only one in our catchment area. They were unable to re-establish the friendships that we'd assumed would still be in place.

I would not want to change for a minute though our choices and experiences, nor those of the boys. They already had a sense of difference and a view of a world bigger than where we happened to be living currently. Jordan enjoyed doing battle with his utterly irreligious teacher. I was proud to hear that my nine year old was standing up to a teacher and more than that, taking the fight to him!

Travelling with families is much harder, and requires more effort

Although my wife and I knew we were back to primarily help with her dying mother, we also keenly felt, that having tasted adventure, we would be off again soon.

I tried to find work. I'd been a successful Financial Controller for a world renowned Pharmaceutical company. Having given all that up to go off and "do" voluntary work, I hadn't really imagined being back again in the rat race.

A local job came up with an NHS Trust. I knew I was qualified, probably overly so, and applied. We had a mortgage to be paid and the family needed stability. I didn't even get an interview, the agency saying I had no NHS experience and too much commercial bias. A week later the agency called me back to see whether I might indeed like to attend for interview. Apparently they had interviewed the NHS experienced candidates and none of them could offer what they were looking for. The role was as Directorate Accountant for the Facilities and Estates Directorate, This was all the non-medical elements that run a hospital, such as grounds, utilities, catering, cleaning, and engineering. I pulled together a quick and easy PowerPoint presentation, having learned from previous disasters of course, preferring to talk than to deliver some fancy presentation. I told them how I'd manage the Finance Team to deliver information that would enable their Managers to make real decisions that would serve the Hospital and enable them to do their health-care work more efficiently. I had the call as soon as I returned home and started a week later.

Having told them what I would do, I had to deliver. Boasting at interview is only good for so long, sooner or later they'd want to see results!

NHS systems are as complex and messy and convoluted as would be expected for such a massive behemoth. I figured I had a few weeks to back up my amazing presentation promises. My Roche days had really helped me to focus on what is truly required, and to block out the multiple incongruous demands and expectations. I worked through my small team's tasks and identified the time consuming elements that added no value to anyone. Essentially, I did this by ensuring that controllable and uncontrollable costs were displayed clearly and that we paid as much attention to the controllable items as possible. Mountains of allocation journals were scrapped and nobody appeared to notice, let alone care. The team could now get out and meet the various department heads and ensure that the real information was processed quickly and accurately. We did more with less.

I also saw opportunities to generate income and met with department heads, those that had this possibility, to encourage them in this regard. If the NHS is required to deliver a 3% saving each year, you can of course cut costs, or increase revenue. One is less painful.

There were monthly Finance department meetings where the five Directorate Accountants and their assistants would report back to the Deputy Head of Finance all the reasons and excuses for poor performance and variances. They would last for hours. Because my team met budget for twenty four consecutive months, my peers may have been a little peeved with my regular and quick five minute update compared to their lengthy grilling!

The Public Sector is not the same as the Private Sector, not by a long way

Grown up Accountants become community members

It will happen. Either you will grow up and realise that you need to make a contribution, or others will seek you out. As an Accountant you are after all a person of stature. There are plenty of studies that suggest the older we get the more we desire to make our mark in things that will endure beyond us. Octogenarians rarely, if ever, wish they could have worked in the office more, rather to have spent time with their family, plus investing in stuff that would live on after them. We, eventually, all want to know we existed and that we mattered.

I'd spent time being the treasurer for my old tennis club, and had been on the PCC at an old church. I'd even been a voluntary worker of course in Jamaica, about as counter cultural as you like. I was not now however thinking about serving my local community.

But, I was getting angry watching Question Time. My sweet wife, getting increasingly frustrated with me shouting at the TV, suggested I either put up or shut up. I proposed to do something and in a slightly childish moment, went on to the internet to fix things!

I was getting cross at what I saw was a European Union (EU) project destined to remove freedom and subjugate us. British law is case law and essentially says there is no law, except if you hurt others, at which time we probably ought to make some rules up. Continental law, or Napoleonic law, essentially says that you as an individual have no rights, except those that the state says you have.

Anyway, I joined the UK Independence Party (UKIP) noticing a banner that said applications for Prospective Parliamentary Candidates closed in an hour. I applied for that too. That would show my wife I was "putting up". This all got rather out of hand, quickly too. I eventually ended up passing the membership interview, applied to become the Eastbourne candidate in a local hustings and found myself on the ballot-paper for the 2005 general election. To say that the next six months were a challenge is a little of an understatement. My personal motivation view was one primarily of sovereignty and freedom, the prevailing press and therefore man-on-the-street view was that I was as bad as the BNP. So I got used to being spat at, sworn at and shouted at whenever I put on my purple tie and rosette. I lost my deposit, but saw first-hand how politics works, or don't, in the UK. Glad I did it, glad it's over, and it was an interesting season of "community service" that I now share carefully!

I'd spent a few years windsurfing off the beach in Eastbourne. We'd taken a conscious decision as a married couple, when we moved to Eastbourne, that we would deliberately explore and enjoy our local area, wherever it was. We were there to live, not just survive. Being so close to the sea, and not being rich enough for a boat, we thought that windsurfing would be a way of enjoying it. We were fortunate enough in our early marriage to buy Ally's best friend's dad's VW camper van. We would park on the beach, Ally would make a cuppa, read and watch the boys play and I'd go out and play too. Lovely.

Fast forward a few years and I'm now forty, returned from Jamaica and attempting to be a grown up. I decided that sailing was a more mature thing to do than windsurfing. I also thought that until I had enough money to buy a boat, I'd at least get trained, so when I had one I'd know what to do with it! Great plan. I took the RYA Day Skipper course through evening classes at the local college and passed with flying colours. Ally then paid for a week long live aboard sailing course, where I would put all this into action and get certified as a competent sailor. Now at age fifty three I still haven't got a boat and my sailing experience can be summarised into just two events.

1. I'd later tell Ally's Cousin Daniel that I'd passed my RYA course and if he wanted help ever, I would love to come down and join him. Daniel had moved out to Italy several years ago and makes

his living managing the boats of the very wealthy. He oversees the maintenance and sail readiness of half a dozen seriously high end boats and gets very well paid for what he loves to do. So, I was hired as crew to sail a million pound Swan 65 from Italy to St Tropez in readiness for a Rolex race, for the wealthy owner and his buddies, who would be playing with it there.

2. On my fourth visit to Malawi, I finally managed to get a couple of days away and we visited Lake Malawi. My host, another Daniel, attempted to redress my complete lack of real sailing experience by sticking me in an antique "Topper" and setting off for a little trip. The story, involving Hippos, comes later!

Being grown up seemed to require money, so I went back to playing at windsurfing. Older and not thinking clearly, and possibly remembering my abilities as they used to be, rather than what they were now, I went to the sea by myself. I repeatedly failed to stand up on the board, almost like something had my board and kept twisting it every time I got on. Eventually, I conceded defeat and ungraciously threw my kit in the back of the car. This was when I noticed the frayed rope holding the mast foot together. I guess it would have lasted for as long as a single long blast out to sea, where it would have failed, leaving me stranded, alone and in rough seas. A lucky escape. I don't think I'm suited to water.

Ally's Mum was stable although her health was failing. Her father in a much better place and coping insofar as he was able to. We'd by now spent two years back in Eastbourne and were getting restless. We knew that with the family situation, it was probably wise to try and stay in the UK but we were also minded to try and make our way in the voluntary, sometimes referred to now as third-sector, world. How could we best use our skills and experience to make a real difference to people's lives, and could we do this in the UK?

Fast forward to today and I now have the privilege of serving as Chair of Trustees for Beachy Head Chaplaincy. This is a local voluntary organisation, patrolling the notorious, infamous chalk cliffs. My role is to work with the trustees and ensure the governance and leadership and management are all in place, efficient and effective. By doing this, we leave the staff and volunteers to patrol up on the head. They do this all year round, in all weathers and often at great personal cost and inconvenience. This is definitely one of those activities that has a measurable impact; every intervention, every search is a chance to literally save lives.

Islanders really do think differently

The job came up and I cannot even recall now where I saw it advertised, as it was really outside my usual sphere. For most of my accounting roles, whether it was me looking for roles or employing people into organisations where I already worked, I would use Hays. My only caveat was that they had to send me a "grown up"! I had long since moved past the stage where I could have a twenty something try to convince me to see or hire their chosen candidate, or else to apply for the special role they'd identified for me. Send me someone who knows how the world works and I can have a meaningful adult conversation with. To their credit they usually did.

The role was Centre Manager for a long established charity's residential activity centre on the Isle of Wight. Close enough for staying in touch with family but far enough away, across the Solent, to be "somewhere".

I did my usual thing of saying hello to the staff in the kitchen on my way through to the interview and that was enough apparently for me to get the seal of approval from them!

I recall reading once the two most important people in any larger company are the caretaker and the cook. They typically don't take any crap from anyone, including CEOs, and know what's going on and can get you access anywhere anytime. Friends will always help you out. I wasn't attempting to manipulate the staff, but simple good manners would mean you'd say hello and meet them, surely?

They asked, after my presentation was over, whether I might consider becoming the Deputy Manager instead of the Centre Manager. They'd obviously been interviewing the current Deputy Manager for the role and had already assigned him the role. I said "yes, sure" as it was in reality the only job on offer. The very fact that they'd asked me this unusual question during my interview meant they'd already determined this was the path of choice. I lined up with it rather than fought it. And, surely, a deputy role would mean an easier role, wouldn't it?

I don't think in hindsight I could have done anything else with regards to the role, but boy was the newly appointed Manager threatened. Bearing in mind my financial background, he kept the budget setting and financial oversight to himself. Anything I suggested he took to a retired friend of his for approval and discussion. My role was effectively cook's assistant, wash-hand, caretaker's assistant and cleaner. That lot took up most of the forty hours a week. In the additional hours I did the book-keeping and drove the minibus, went shopping for food supplies and the various practical jobs you might expect for a 52 week, 24/7 one hundred and thirty bed youth activity centre. I added Lifeguard to my CV and list of life accomplishments. I was the oldest by a decade or two on the course, and barely made it through the swimming timed tests!

My CV and LinkedIn profile said I took this slight career meander to "help broaden my overall not-for-profit experience". True enough if truth is spelt with a small "t". Having one weekend off in three, and for the first time in my entire career having disciplinary conversations with my superior, made it clear that (a) this role wasn't me and (b) I would not be working for this Manager any longer than I had to.

If you're not fulfilled it shows

I'd had to have a minor overnight hospital procedure on my nose, which necessitated some quite strong steroids to help the healing process. I was, rather nonchalantly in retrospect, warned there might be some side effects, such as feeling hungry and mild irritability.

We'd planned a week's holiday off the island and there was a major water leak the night before we left, which I left in the capable hands of the resident maintenance guy. Apparently this amounted to dereliction of duty according to the Centre Manager. Unfortunately in having decided to wait until my return from holiday, he'd coincided my disciplinary chat with my being on the steroids; he chosen the wrong moment for confrontation.

Sitting me in a large room directly opposite him, with a long list of complaints written down, he proceeded to warn me about my behaviour and performance. Responding to him, I could hear the words coming out of my mouth. Although possibly perfectly polite I was extremely strongly worded, but I simply didn't care. It wasn't that I was irritable, that in no way came near to how angry I was. I could hear the words, knew that I'd never usually say those things or in that way, but was quite enjoying the moment. Steroids are nature's way of taking the "passive" out of passive aggressive. I might add that the list of "complaints" were a complete surprise and basically he didn't like my attitude, nor me. He brought up the fact that I'd gone after his job at the interview and he still wasn't happy.

I've been in some seriously high pressure roles before and only on two occasions in a thirty year career have I had to have a "chat" with a superior, and one of those was with a crook suggesting I break the law if I "knew what was good for me". The other instance, of course, where my MD had deliberately concealed truth from his US boss.

Human Resources from Headquarters got involved and it was suggested that I might like to have some career counselling. I took it. The charity didn't really know how to manage this situation and just wanted it all to go away. I'm not too sure whether there was a life lesson or principle to be gleaned from all this? Maybe it's simply that charities have a long way to go in professionalising their people management? Maybe, maybe not. Maybe one simply comes across people in power from time to time that shouldn't be there, that you are sometimes powerless, or maybe that you can't get on with everyone all the time. There was obviously nothing I could do about the situation. So I had to put up with it, or move elsewhere.

The legislative changes meaning retirement ages are no longer enforceable also meant that there was no end in sight to the Centre Manager's tenure. This in hindsight was the motivation we needed and so we decided to properly consider a move back into the adventurous world we'd left behind in Jamaica.

I'd also received an invitation from Cousin Daniel to do a yacht delivery with him in the Mediterranean. The centre manager, who also enjoyed sailing, but never found the time to do it, managed to find a reason for explicitly not allowing me any time off at all anywhere near the suggested dates. He may have been jealous. It further added to my growing list of reasons for leaving.

Looking back, what did I learn, was it a beneficial season? Well, yes. We had the time, away from the usual elements of modern living, to consider our long term desires. We also took the decision to home-school our boys. One perk of this residential job was a four bedroom detached lodge set in twenty eight acres of grounds, and someone else to cut the grass! We now had the time, space and a home set up to explore the future.

Home-Schooling, a new adventure

Unusually, there was a really strong and vibrant home-school community on the island. Island communities, we later learned, tend to attract "differently minded" souls. Back in Eastbourne, there might have been half a dozen home-school families in the whole town. Here on the island (with a similar population) there was enough for several schools. In this community different parents would offer up different skills as their contribution. Some did maths coaching, some a football club, one was a Chef who taught a cookery class. It was sweet to learn that the UK has laws dating back centuries that mean parents are legally responsible for educating their children. Furthermore, the state has no place intervening, except if they feel the child is coming to harm. We had families from as far away as Germany coming to the UK, away from places where governments were taking children into care. The proof of their parental unsuitability being as simple as to think they could provide an education different to or better than the state. We gave the boys cards saying that they were home-schooled, should the Police or anyone ever stop them. They had freedom to study as they wanted, and go out as they wanted. Once they started to own their own learning, it was amazingly liberating. I even managed to spend time with Jordan and work through him being able to understand Maths.

Home-schooling gave us the freedom to tailor the day and the learning entirely for their benefit. We were not anti-school, but saw an opportunity to help shape our sons' lives directly. We'd grown accustomed to their company and all the research and evidence we'd seen had suggested it works. We had the example of our Canadian friends' children out in Jamaica as role models for the entire process too.

It also meant that for the next stage of our lives, we'd be able to travel wherever we wished, whenever we wished, with the freedom for us to do this as a family unit, together.

Joel our youngest, only spent his primary years at "normal" school, and some of that in Jamaica. He's now studying for a Masters in Civil Engineering. Jordan, had more time in conventional education, and we made all the mistakes with him, being the eldest and therefore first! He's currently in Beijing studying Mandarin. We like to think that home-schooling worked for them.

I went to play on the sea, again

I went sailing. I'd bought a small 16' dinghy off EBay, found an old two stroke outboard and borrowed a leaking rubber dingy. Possibly being an "overner" was the reason I had trouble getting people to teach me. Ages later, and in desperation one evening, I thought "how hard can it really be?" Motoring out from Bembridge the Solent was smooth; I rounded the headland right into a huge chop.

For "safety" I kept the engine ticking over as I threw the sail up, carelessly leaving the trailing edge of the rope hanging out the back. It took about a second for the main "sheet" to be pulled into the motor. I was now with a fully sheeted-in sail, in the wind, but with no steering and was properly stuffed. I desperately hung over the back of the boat trying to unwind the rope, the boat bobbing badly and now drifting into the shipping channels. After about twenty minutes I managed to free the rope and start the engine. Phew. Immediately the boom smacked into my head, nearly knocking me out the boat. Dazed, I did eventually manage to somehow get myself back to harbour.

I sold the boat on EBay the next week and I was very careful how I shared with Mrs M, a long time later.

I have now had to promise her that I will only venture out onto the sea if I have a suitably qualified and competent "grown up" with me.

Be deliberate about keeping hold of your dreams

Colorado, the big dream; combining work, calling and family

At this point, one might be forgiven in thinking that we've had it pretty good so far. I had been a qualified Accountant, earning well and giving it all up out of choice. We had moved to the Caribbean for a couple of years and now after two years back home, had then spent a further two years ostensibly out of the rat race again on the Isle of Wight which was itself an escape for some. We were now heading off to Colorado, hardly a tough place to live!

We'd started to think about a development sphere and because we were people of faith, also "missions" work. Some countries and cultures react differently to the title "missionary". For us, knowing that financial management was the area I would work in, "charity worker" sometimes suited better. It also depends on your audience. To our church friends, our role would be missionary, to neighbours and friends, NGO voluntary worker. To our family, we would be charity workers. Having Ally as a qualified teacher at least meant that their tendency to think we were ruining our boy's lives through the medium of home-education, was to some extent, ameliorated. What we did though would be exactly the same. I would use my finance and management experience and skills to help charities perform better and stay operating and effective for longer. Ally would use her people skills to help mend broken people, so they could perform better and for longer.

From our previous experiences, we knew that family involvement in many international development NGOs meant we would have trouble securing a role. I also was keen on the voluntary aspect, actually getting involved at the lower levels of society for a season to see what impact we might be able to make. I wanted to move away from yet another corporate job, which I thought even a large NGO might become. Longer term, a season at the sharp end would mean that should I ever return to such a senior management role, I'd know what successful implementation and delivery looked like.

It was almost like proper career planning, of sorts!

For Ally, with her school teaching qualifications and experience, it was an easy fit; she'd turn up and her skills would be universally needed and welcomed. She also has this gift of getting alongside the broken and the prickly and transforming their sense of well-being. She'd given away her clothes, prayed for people in the street, visited aids patients, attended inquests with people and fed the mentally ill on the streets of Montego Bay. She'd also made bricks with her bare hands in Zambia and dug trenches to lay power cables to a remote hospital. Allegedly she'd also learnt to kill a chicken and cook it from scratch, although she still won't touch spiders.

Researching, now for a second time with more knowledge and experience, lead us to YWAM, the global Christian voluntary organisation. Every new volunteer is required to undergo a very similar six month internship and training programme. This essentially instils the same set of values across every worker in every one of their 1,000+ locations and projects. They also deliver this training specifically aimed at families and the less-young volunteers! We decided on Colorado Springs, they had a programme that catered for the boys, indeed welcomed them, were based in the wilderness of Colorado, and their focus of operations was the 10/40 world.

[The 10/40 Window is the rectangular area of North Africa, the Middle East and Asia approximately between 10 degrees north and 40 degrees north latitude. The 10/40 Window is home to the majority of the world's poor. Of the poorest of the poor, more than eight out of ten live in the 10/40 Window. On average, they exist on less than a few hundred dollars per person per year.]

Source: Wikipedia, Joshua Project et al.

Personal faith in public action

My wife is a great and faithful friend. She decided a long time ago that friends are like plants; unloved and untended, they tend to wither and die. She was determined not to lose the quality people she has come across over the years so sets out to deliberately stay in touch.

She won't get this far through the book so I can say this without her being embarrassed; she also does a similar thing for many strangers she comes across as well as those she knows to be lonely and friendless, although she does this anonymously. She determines to be a blessing to one person every day of her life. This might mean dropping off a card or a plant outside someone's door. Sometimes its cash, or a gift card. Sometimes she spends time praying for them. She might write a letter, drop an email, send a Facebook message or make that telephone call. In the past month, she's been encouraging friends over skype and Facebook, in Asia and Canada.

What this means is that we have friends all over the world! I get to receive the benefits of her many years of labour. So, I surprised her, ensuring our flights to Colorado went through Montreal which meant we could spend a few nights visiting her best friend from school before we started our new season. The price difference was less than a tenner, perfect, almost a sensible choice then.

Invest in friendships – consciously & deliberately

Back in the classroom as a forty-something, humbling but good

Our training included a theological understanding of the basis for what missionaries do and why they do it. Actually, I think it would work even if you did it with no faith! Let me explain, although please forgive me, if in my assessment of a secular worldview, I might inadvertently horrify anyone who has properly studied these things!

A secularist or humanist might say that "these people" deserve help, or have a right to it, or that it makes one feel good to do it. All well and good. But what happens when they reject your offer of help, spit in your face, try to kill you? A Christian worldview would say that the imprint of God is in everyone, and God himself deserves the recognition of this fact in every person. This bypasses or transcends my personal feelings and provides me with a higher motivation that enables me to cope with all the bad shit that eventually and typically, inevitably comes.

One of the places in India we were to visit several months later was infamous locally for being where an Australian missionary family was locked in their car and burnt alive. A slightly wishy washy feeling that these people deserve our kindness may not have worked.

A few years later I'd find myself in Switzerland, watching Joel, my youngest, play Rugby for the local Nyon side; standing next to a United Nations (UN) worker. I thought I'd ask about his view on the work the UN does, as YWAM and UN have sometimes clashed at a local level, from what some of our colleagues said. Genuinely seeking a positive endorsement from this insider, I was taken aback by his downbeat response. Essentially, he and his colleagues recognised that truly, only people of faith – of which he had none – could stand in the places of most need. With no faith, it was all simply too overwhelming.

In the training, most of the people in authority over me were half my age. I chose to humble myself and take their instruction, no matter what I thought of their style or ability! YWAM tend to place the young in impossible situations and see them succeed, or fail, knowing that most organisations would never do this. It's called taking risks. They have had some spectacular success stories.

For example, we'd later learn of the history of some of our friends, working in Thailand in the early eighties, in the Cambodian refugee crisis. They turned up to help and were told rather dismissively that they could clean up the human waste, which was reaching waist high levels, and that nobody would or could fix. They decided to go ahead and serve and do the best they could and eventually they cleaned up the mess. Many years later, and when the Tsunami hit in 2004, one of the first calls made by the Thai authorities was to our friends; they could be trusted to do whatever needed to be done.

Many or most world changers started their careers really young. Modern day examples include Richard Branson, Bill Gates, Steve Jobs, and Mother Theresa. If you read the early accounts of their careers, one might be forgiven for not seeing "brilliance" so easily.

Now before everyone gets uppity about "evangelism" and shoving things down people's throats; YWAM adopt a model whereby they ask people what their needs are and seek to meet them first (the UN tell people what their needs are and deliver that). The hope is that they would then have earned the right to answer the question "why are you doing this". They also tend to go in as a learner, to uncover what aspect of the glory of God is displayed in this or that particular people group or tribe. It's an easy model to sign up to.

Good friends of ours had lived in Nepal and Tibet for a season several years ago. As well as living amongst the people there, they also researched the well-known issues of people trafficking and the poverty that fuels this evil trade. They heard of one village where all the girls and young women between ten and thirty simply weren't there anymore, they'd all been trafficked, or sold or sent off to cities to earn a living. Arriving at the village required a climb down a waterfall, a little like the film "The Mission" but not quite as dramatic.

They met with the village elders and asked if they could work with them to create a tourism enterprise. Five14Nepal.com is a local Kathmandu based tourism business and it sustains itself as well as enabling local businesses to employ local people.

They helped build a couple of lodges where guests could sleep, taught them how to cook and not kill the tourists, helped them understand the value they had all around them (Red Panda for example close by) and even helped introduce the making of small craft items which Five14 would sell in the city.

The hope was that a small sustainable business might help to start the process of bringing wealth into their community and thereby provide opportunities so that the girls wouldn't have to move away. The reality was that in just six months, the elders came to them and said they'd met and decided that there was so much income and activity in the village, they would no longer would send any girls away. A teacher even came back to the village and opened the school again.

Success; through vision, dedication and appropriate help.

We also learned that Americans do not share the same sense of humour as we do. They tend to find it difficult to laugh at themselves. I shan't dwell on this, except to say it caused several very uncomfortable situations, and we slowly learned to modify our naturally brilliantly funny British sense of humour! We learnt that maybe Brits are a little too sarcastic, and underplayed dryness can be met with tumbleweed and embarrassed silence...

Humour is universal, but it is also very cultural

Our three months classroom and community living experience were done with. Yes, community living. Rather like the army, community living, serving, chores, getting up early to help everyone else, is hard wired into the "curriculum" because they know it brings up all our crap and self-sufficiency and brings it to the surface! Oh joy. There's nothing quite like living and sleeping and working and studying in very close proximity to a set of flawed human beings that will bring out the very worst in your character. Dealing with these things in the relative safety of a community serves to make us hopefully more rounded people. It also prepared us for the challenges of living cross culturally in a "development situation".

And, by the way, if you're reading this, you are really one of the 1%

India, it is very different

I'd of course done the foreign travel, with a multinational company, before. Taxi to the airport, business lounge, choice of seats, direct flights, decent quality hotels where you stay, taxis and drivers, food and fixers. Not forgetting tourist activities and fancy restaurants for when you are done with the working day. Lovely food and the best places. You get a type of cultural experience without any of the crap that most people in that particular culture have to put up with. It's very enticing, it's enjoyable and one of the reasons why I chose only international companies in my job searches a few years ago.

This was however, quite different.

Our role in India was to work alongside a charity called "Dinbandhu" or friend of the poor. The clue is in the name. When I say "work", in essence we were mainly there to provide an attraction that would draw attention to the agency and therefore legitimacy for the many local charity workers who did the day to day hard graft.

International business has a social, local impact and cost

I'd read a piece in the Sunday papers before we went to the US, it was an analysis of a letter Prince Charles had written, exposing the problems with genetically modified seeds in the developing world. He'd been typically vilified by the press in the UK, but this reporter decided to dig deeper. The actual situation was worse than even Price Charles had made out. Apparently the Genetically Modified (GM) company let's call them "Inc." had obtained an agreement from the Indian government to be the sole supplier of seed to the nation. Unfortunately, GM food requires at least twice the normal volume of water. It is also engineered barren so you can't then use the output to save and grow your own food next year. You have to keep coming back. And it's more expensive than traditional seed. So, when the rains fail, many hundreds of farmers lose their crops, are made bankrupt and in a society with no hope, commit suicide.

We attended one event, put on by Dinbandhu, for the widows and orphans in Maharashtra region. They put out seating for five thousand and made such a fuss and noise that the event reached the ears of central government, who sent a minister of state to attend. It was a remarkable event, simply ministering to the poorest of the poor would make national news and hopefully change government policy.

Out away from town we were like celebrities; many if not most of the residents in the villages had never seen a foreigner, and definitely not foreign children. The team would get up and share some simple truth or life experience and the crowds would turn up to listen. At schools and orphanages, even my two boys would get up and address the crowds. All the time, the excitement we created meant that the local workers, who were there day in and day out, had extra impact and street-cred, legitimacy, for the work they did.

The boys and I stood on a street corner just for fun one day. We did nothing else than stand and chat amongst ourselves. In less than ten minutes we had a crowd of around fifty people asking for autographs, posing for photographs and staring at our faces from inches away. Personal space is not an Indian concept!

We took part in the actual delivery of many hundreds of "Shoebox Christmas Gifts". Many schools and organisations in the UK create shoebox gift boxes to send off around the world. I often wondered what happened to them; well, we handed out a couple of thousand! They were the only material things that many of the children would have.

We were invited to a wedding. Our host said we'd not be required to contribute anything as our presence alone, as foreigners, would bring their friend's family enormous honour in their village. The village had three chairs for the wedding, one of which the bride's mother gave up for me. I had to take it, it brought her honour to sit on the ground and for me to sit on the chair. I cannot even begin to say what that felt like, even whether it was right or wrong, but sometimes you do have to take the local advice and go with the flow.

Halfway through the ceremony I was told that as the guest of honour, I'd be expected to say a few words to the bride and groom and attending crowd, now even larger due to presence of foreign guests. We'd been in India long enough now to guess that even when they explicitly say "no speeches", they really mean "speech every time". I so wanted to say "and now you may kiss the bride" but managed to contain myself. I later learned that the appropriate custom locally is that the bride must be seen to be distraught at the prospect of leaving her mother to go with this man and it is not a time of celebration, kissing the groom would be completely out of the question!

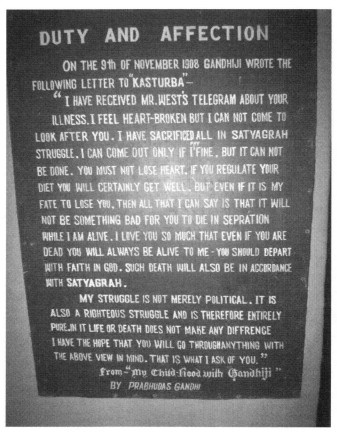

We did learn that we were not in control of our destiny for that couple of months. The less we struggled the easier it was.

We were invited to go and view another orphanage project, this time for disabled children. Ally was sick again, well actually she'd had diarrhoea for pretty much every day we were there and was dehydrated and in no place to sit in a car for several hours. Jordan had his only bout of sickness in the entire time, his constitution is remarkably buoyant, and so stayed with mum. Joel came with me.

Culturally, men are still in charge. Smita, who was the actual, and female, Director in charge of a hundred or so workers, became my interpreter for the day, as those we met just deferred to me as being in charge. She knew of course this would happen and would graciously accept these situations when appropriate. I was therefore now, for the day at least, Director in charge of all the many and varied good works of Dinbandhu! As guests of honour, we were given a dish of food to eat, before they all ate later, and in full view of everyone. There were so many flies on the plate that you literally couldn't physically see the food at all. The only thing to do was to move your hand in, grab a handful, hope that all the flies would depart, leaving you with only food to place into your mouth. I can't tell whether that worked, but I think I got my protein intake that day in what was a generally vegetarian environment.

Another trip, this time to an orphanage for blind children. We learned that although a few may have been deliberately blinded in order to beg, most were there due to a simple vitamin deficiency in the mothers, meaning the children's eyes didn't develop properly in the womb. The 99% on less than a $1/day. Sad doesn't even begin to cover it.

It was humbling to understand that we had no skills they required, except our pretty western faces to draw a crowd.

India could also be amazing, colourful and fun. The people were generous and kind. Beggars though were often aggressive. Ally would take sweets to hand out to the children. That way they got a small benefit and it wouldn't be taken away by their handlers.

Our first day in Delhi, laughably helping us to acclimatise to the environment, was a shock to the system. Jamaica had slums and we had visited families living literally on the city dump. They were wealthy and healthy in comparison.

Our hotel for our first two nights was a concrete box in amongst other concrete boxes, in the company of various half-naked men parading around, spitting and smoking, and generally staring at us. It was hot, forty degrees hot and the power went out for hours at a time. It was also very humid. Everything was damp and sweaty and dark and smelly and not at all pleasant.

There were enough of us in our team to fill three Tuk-Tuks and we were going to go to a McDonalds, mainly so our American team members would feel at home, as it had air condition (a/c). Apparently there were several such establishments all within a few minutes of our "hotel"; what followed resembled a Benny Hill high-speed farcical chase scene. We dashed off in three different directions and zoomed off to one McDonalds, saw that nobody was there, and dashed off to another, and finally all ended up arriving at one location at the same time about an hour later. Whether it was the intended destination was by now irrelevant. There weren't any burgers on the menu, but there was a/c and it even had queues; queueing is apparently one unintended American export delivered through the medium of McDonald's restaurants.

Medicines are freely available in the larger towns, and most people self-diagnose. Apparently the timing or our diarrhoea bouts would determine which particular bug was the cause and this would mean a particular type of solution. Antibiotics were cheaper than penny sweets. We made our own yoghurt, by placing some in a container of milk, leaving it on the side all day and the fridge overnight. We'd then sprinkle some kind of special powder on this and our guts would be re-set for the new day. This would be fine until we ate something else and would get the shits again. Jordan and Joel had one day of illness each, my wife had maybe one day when she wasn't ill.

Sometimes, you simply have to let go, and swim with the tide

Toilet humour

I knew things had got bad when Mrs M was sitting on the toilet one day and casually pulled a large cockroach from out of her hair, without even a murmur. It was that routine and she was that tired, it simply didn't even register anymore.

The room that was to be our home for two months was large enough for a double bed and two singles, with a tiny bathroom just off of it. Mattresses were very thin, hard and made of straw. As we were on a corridor accessible to the public, if the door was ajar, Mrs M had to be fully and appropriately, sensitively and ethnically clothed. No a/c, electricity for half the day, 100% humidity and forty+ Celsius. The bathroom bucket was also our "washing machine".

Apparently, the previous lady guest was sitting on the toilet one day when a rat popped its head up to say hello.

We went through villages where there was no sanitation. The custom was to walk to the roadside, squat and perform your business, of whichever number designation, and then go back into the fields. Shit and piss everywhere.

I didn't train as an auditor, many accountants will. One of my early bosses said that as an auditor they graded each of their clients by reference to their toilet facilities. They developed their own auditor version of a "good toilet guide". India would have presented them with a challenge. Another wedding, this time in town, with a proper inside public toilet. Quite how there came to be shit on the ceiling I simply don't know.

Going home

We all voted to spend what little cash we had left and to fly back to Delhi to catch the long flight back to the USA. We'd not all universally enjoyed the overnight train journey from Delhi to Nagpur just two months previously! My two boys thought it was great fun, as they were small enough to hide away on the third tier of the swing-down bed and watch the chaos beneath them. The hole in the floor that made for the toilet and the breakfast brought round by the Chai-Walla were highlights for them. Hours of noise, and smell and being squashed up against strangers, sitting on your luggage so it wouldn't get stolen and screaming children for company had soured the romantic train journey we sometimes imagine this sort of trans-continental event to be!

We'd been warned that however clean we'd tried to be, we'd probably all have worms or some other parasites. Horror stories from one old friend of nearly starving on some African adventure but also having a tape worm inside him, which would then come up his throat looking for food, didn't help. I told my wife it wasn't true. I sort of hoped it wasn't, but, how cool would it be if it were true?

I'd decided to forewarn my boys that our time in India might be a little less holiday-like than what their friends in the UK might be experiencing that summer. We went to India in the full-on heat of July and August. I explained that in order to have a story to tell, you likely have to go through an event that's worth telling, which usually means bad stuff happens. They embraced this a little too keenly I thought; every time some kind of disaster befell the group they'd smile approvingly and say, "oh good, another story".

So, on our last day, sitting at the airport in Delhi, with clean t-shirts bought at the airport, in case we all smelled, I took them to the toilet. I casually explained that I needed to go through their poos and make sure there were no little critters moving around. I took a photo that they still have. It's funny, that such a small visual aid brings memories of India flooding back for them years later! I have a lovely photograph, proof of this tiny story, but it's been banned by the Mrs.

We arrived back in Colorado and hit the showers. We washed the clothes immediately, and then washed them again. We put on the clean clothes that we had left behind in storage. We still smelled of India. We threw our old clothes away. We took another shower.

One of the keenest and weirdest memories was visiting Ghandi's Ashram on the way back from some visit somewhere. Such a cool place; a serious world changer and a real strange guy. His poor wife suffered much! We also got to see the Taj Mahal, so hot though and the unhelpful congruence of religion and history did taint the experience a little.

Back in the USA, we were now officially trained staff and could go anywhere in the world for any YWAM project and they'd know who we were, what we'd been through to get there and had at least a knowledge of the shared values of the organisation.

I'd summarise that six months in three words; toilets, training & trials.

Values & Principles versus Rules & Laws

Modern westerners, I think it's true to say, love rules and shortcuts. Do this, get that, it's all very transactional. Say this thing, achieve that result. In order to get things, there then ends up being a lot of rules to accompany every situation, and new ones keep arising.

Just look at the books in airport shops and the titles on the best seller lists, they're inundated with the latest secret to success and fulfilment and liberation. They sell precisely because we want to distil their apparent, alleged "success" directly into our own lives, with the least inconvenience possible.

Values and principles although harder to keep to, are inherently simpler to understand. For example, "love others". If we truly love others, we place their needs above ours. You don't then need a whole series of rules to govern how we interact. For example in YWAM, they have one value which is "Do first, then teach".

I've translated this into my professional career. So, I try not to ask any of my staff to do a task that I've not done myself at some stage. That might then mean that I have to get my hands dirty in helping carry and sort files into the underground storage, before I can ask them to. I find this a useful aid to successful leadership generally.

Having written this, I am however reminded that in my current role, I have yet to venture down into the basement archives; a job for next week then!

Leadership lesson

The Burmese are short, and Accountants selfish

As we went through a short de-brief process, we began to look again at the opportunities to help around us. The Colorado Springs community helped support and provide the back-office functions for a couple of hundred voluntary workers across many of the 10/40 countries. We'd later see TV news reports of western doctors and health professionals being kidnapped and shot or beheaded in Afghanistan, and then learnt they were part of our community. We'd several single girls, not men, working in countries next to the Taliban. They were that committed to educating girls, stopping trafficking and abuse, that they'd deliberately put themselves in harm's way. They weren't exactly living the ex-pat dream.

For all these hundreds of workers, all mostly living off voluntary donations or self-employed businesses, there was not a single accountant. I saw my opportunity to serve.

Anyone with a heart to make a difference can survive for a short time. Longer term involvement and bringing people in to help, both require longer term investment, places to stay, transportation, and resources. These have to be managed. I could see a tangible result to my efforts; systems and administration meant that these workers and volunteers could stay for the long term. Long term consistent involvement is the key to long term results.

We returned to the UK with a fresh vision of what we would do. So started a fresh visa process and over the next couple of months we began to tell our story and asked whether people might like to contribute towards what we were going to be doing.

Having a clear vision is key

We shared with family and friends. Knowing what the community in Colorado was involved with made it an easy vision to sell. There were some jealous of our seemingly envious lifestyle. It was interesting though, the most vocal challenges were more to do with the fact that we had managed to leave the rat race and it wasn't fair on them as they had to stay.

They had no clue about the sacrifices. Try living in community. Try living off food banks, or hoping you won't get sick, or need the dentist, because you can't afford health insurance. It's been said that nothing truly worthwhile is easy to achieve. I would echo that.

We managed to obtain a six month visitor visa to the USA, which was delivered by courier on the Sunday morning, literally the day before we left for the airport. Stressful doesn't come anywhere near describing the events of that particular week, nor our first real engagement with US bureaucracy.

For your career, being deliberate and focused is crucial

One can drift for weeks and months and these turn into years. Just ask anyone in their forties how they ended up where they are now, and then ask them whether they are happy or fulfilled. Time drifts by more quickly the older you get. Inertia builds up imperceptibly. Change is harder to manage the older you get. Be deliberate. Take time out and write down your personal vision. Where do you want to be? Who do you want to be? What do you want to achieve, where do you want to live. Who do you want to marry? Think on these things, write down the answers, and keep referring back to them.

This is the advice I wish most someone could have shared with me when I was young.

Back in Colorado Springs

We arrived back in time for Christmas. Mrs M was ill on the plane and spent the first week in bed, exhausted and bleeding heavily. We hoped rest would sort her out and mostly it did, eventually, sort of.

We were by now living in a half empty former hotel, and had bashed three hotel rooms together to make our apartment.

Some of our team had got involved with helping Burmese refugees. Unaccompanied refugee Minors (URMs) from Burma had been accepted by the state of Colorado but some had nowhere to stay. Our community offered to house them, and we became sort of house-parents. Being from the Chin state, and the Shan tribe, among the poorest of Myanmar's citizens, they were all tiny, especially when lined up alongside our growing boys!

We heard first hand their stories of brutality from the army, escape, and death of siblings on the journey down through Burma, into Thailand and across into Malaysia and finally to Kuala Lumpur and into the UN refugee programme. Most of them were just young teenagers when they started these journeys, all by themselves. We loved them and tried to be there as much as they needed us to be. They were mostly very worldly wise and a lot more mature than the government, which was helpful but very much a "nanny state", gave them credit for. They'd seen stuff, had travelled thousands of miles, across borders, by themselves with no money and no papers. They were now considered "children" once more and had a lot less freedom!

We had great fun with them and helped, as much as we could, for example getting bank accounts, driving licences and ferrying them around to see their other friends.

A test for Accountants

Try to explain to someone who has never had a bank account, why a bank account is better and safer than using cash. One of the girls, very trusting of her new American friends, had her bank account emptied the first week.

We undertook training of potential new field workers. Two years of living in Jamaica put us in a very small group of people that had lived overseas, or had lived life as a volunteer. I oversaw the finances and put the charity, which had a substantial amount of money flowing through it, through two successful audits and statutory inspections, for the very first time!

We valued living amongst people who shared a common vision. We learnt about different worldviews; hope is a somewhat rare spiritual aspect to Christianity that appears very little in most other world religions.

It was startling to realise, for me at least, that the 1% secular west is not the whole world. Most people, in most countries and the majority of the world's population, are spiritual beings and see the world through a spiritual set of glasses. We do well to remember that in our relatively small, by comparison, western bubble.

Vision translates into any business too. I recall that the Managing Director (MD) at Roche would announce a problem or some fresh challenge and the senior team would all volunteer to help and to collaborate to overcome it. It was an inspiring place to work.

We were told to come over on a six month tourist visa and they would help switch it into a ten year business visa. Unbelievably, especially when I recount our Jamaican experience, we took them at their word. It's not that they were dishonest, they just assumed competence in an area in which they had none. Part of the consequence of promoting young people to positions of leadership!

Matters were not helped when we didn't spot the immigration officer not being able to count to six and only giving us five months to stay. The US Visa is simply permission to travel to a port of entry and request permission to enter – we learned.

Legal advice suggested that as we were "in process", departing now would render the process null and void and we'd have to start again. That re-commencement would then be from outside the country and with a potential overstay on our record. We seemed committed to staying. The legal advice given to us was that transitioning into an "overstay" and have the permission back-dated is typically what happens.

During this time, the tenants in our house back in Eastbourne had departed. Having decided to commit to staying in the US, and with rental income barely covering the mortgage and maintenance costs, we chose to sell the house. Things went very badly wrong very quickly indeed! The agents didn't like selling with tenants, and we had a succession of short term tenants and some that ended up not paying. The housing market started to slide, and we lost a third of the value in the house. We did eventually sell the house, but for much less than we wanted, and then the buyer fell out, meanwhile, there were no tenants.

A second sale fell through several weeks later. Meanwhile we had a mortgage to be paid and no income to cover it. Someone said that fasting in these circumstances would help. Fasting is present in many cultures, for well-known ancient health reasons as well as for spiritual direction.

I reluctantly decided to start a three day, total abstention from food, fast. Someone, very helpfully, then said that seven days is a "spiritually" whole number, someone else later suggested ten days. Then yet another helpful person said that the most famous fasting of all, Daniel, was for twenty one days. As the hunger and appetite had basically disappeared after the second or third day, and I was still functioning as normal, I foolishly said I'd fast until the house sold. By now the boys had got bored of waving doughnuts under my nose as it had no impact. Our house did in fact sell on the twenty first day. Yet another helpful person said it might be worth "sealing the deal" with another three days. And so ended a twenty four day fast. It is possible to abstain from food in the right circumstances. It may all have all been an amazing coincidence of course.

The house sold and we cleared the mortgage with about £4,000 to spare. By now we had got used to living "poorly" and decided to invest the house proceeds. We bought the boys a MacBook each for their educational investment and decided to invest £1,000 into the Indian project we'd been working with. One of the villages we visited lost half its houses and farm animals when a fire burnt everything. They weren't able to extinguish the fire as they were a three km walk to the nearest water. Our relatively modest gift would be enough to pay for a well to be drilled and installed. We considered it an eternal investment! Mrs M allowed me to spend the remaining cash on a motorbike, rather than anything sensible, sensing I needed it! I spent many an evening and weekend on an XR400 dirt bike riding the playground that is the Rocky Mountains. I just had to watch out for Mountain Lions and Brown Bears, which was fine so long as you didn't stop for long!

Don't trust anyone who says "don't worry it'll be easy"

Far from being a disaster, which on some grounds this obviously was, it was liberating. No house to worry about meant we could move freely and had less worries. You know you can't take anything with you, we were starting to live that particular truth more consciously than ever. For several years, apart from whichever vehicle we happened to be driving, my most expensive possessions were a pair of tennis rackets and my adventure Casio watch, none of which cost more than a hundred quid or so.

This was, for us, Freedom

Best toilet story ever

Some of the menfolk, yes I was used to living and talking American by now, had got together for some food and hanging out. There was, unusually, beer. Some Americans are unusually uptight on alcohol, as are many Christians around the world, possibly due to a deposited sense of appropriateness from either old fashioned Methodist views or recent American church cultures. Anyway, I digress. Alcohol can liberate the tongue and we were all swapping stories. I mentioned the toilet situation in rural India, and then Scotty stepped in with his.

He and some friends had been helping in Haiti. The toilet installed at their accommodation was a "drop-toilet" the like of which we'd seen in several places in the Caribbean. It's a toilet seat on a platform, which sits over a massive empty fibreglass container. Deposits are made, insects and bacteria take care of partially decomposing the detritus and it's all kept out of the local community gardens, roads and water table. Simple and nice. I never found out what happens if they ever fill up.

One night, their friend went out to perform a number two. There being no electricity, he took a torch. It was dark outside and pitch black inside. He heard some movement and then scared himself witless when he saw a large spider rather too close to where he was sitting. He screamed loudly and then stood up on the toilet rim to get away from the spider. Spiders in Haiti are big. However, he then misjudged how we was standing and he then slipped down and into the toilet itself and got himself well and truly wedged at the waist. He frantically screamed out some more, this time for help. His brave friends came running when they heard the noise and couldn't of course help themselves laughing at the sight. Funny enough if the story ended there. Scotty paused a short while for dramatic effect.

They then proceeded to try and extract him from the mess he'd gotten himself into. Laurel and Hardy style, they ended up standing either side of the toilet, taking hold of him under the arms and started to pull up as hard as they could. Now, the toilet is moulded and stuck separately onto the top of the large receptacle. The weight and motion of three grown men placed too much strain on the joints and welds and the whole lot snapped and they ended up twisting and falling head-first into the mess below. Try and imagine that early scene from Slumdog Millionaire. Several visits to hospital and injections ensued. We decided that Scotty's story won.

YWAM is a mainly youth-led and staffed organisation. Being American, the men were manly men. Leisure pursuits sometimes meant trying to keep up with blokes half my age. In the summer, Colorado turn ski slopes into downhill mountain bike tracks. I'd inadvertently already done some "blue" fast sections involving actual proper jumps but had now come to a standstill whilst we negotiated our way over some rocks. From a standing start I manged to lock my front wheel in a rock, somersault over the bars and dive headfirst onto a rock. Being knocked unconscious I didn't even hear the bang as my helmet exploded from the impact. My companions all thought I'd died. The $15 helmet, bought the evening before, had taken the impact about ¼" from my exposed temple. It didn't help that when I woke up and was taken to the medical centre to be checked out, one of the group called his wife and told her they thought I'd killed myself. She happened to be having afternoon tea with Mrs M. Oops.

Family Expedition to Asia – in-between jobs!

Ally's mum had passed away, and her Dad had met and was about to marry Jeannie. We flew back for the big day. I knew instinctively that a visit out of the US to the UK would render all our visa application hard work and sacrifices null and void, and in all likelihood we'd never return. We packed up our apartment, handed the keys to the manager saying we'd be away for at least six months, and asked "was there anyone who wanted a paid for and furnished apartment overlooking Pikes Peak Mountain?" Lookup either Top gear or America's Mountain to see what a great deal this was!

I packed up all the possessions that we might want to come back to and put them into storage. We then stuffed all the personal things we knew we couldn't do without into suitcases to take with us. It was tough to simply give away the apartment, all the furniture and the "stuff" that makes a home. We'd worked so hard to physically turn three standard hotel rooms into a coherent space. I wonder if the kitchen walls are still the lime green colour we chose.

The wedding went well, we enjoyed seeing everyone, but were now in a hiatus. The US visa process was still ongoing and might take several more months. What to do.

We'd made many connections into Asia over the recent few years and knew of several places that were in desperate need for financial and management help. I drew up a plan for a six month trip across Asia. The only fixed item on the agenda was the first couple of days in Bangkok and return flights from Australia some six or seven months later. We'd fill in the gaps as we went and as plans got firmed up, other details would emerge. One of the things that we learnt about voluntary groups such as YWAM was that they don't make plans in the same way. Once they know, for certain, that you will be with them and that it's really going to happen next week, then they'll engage. Before then however, even they might not know what they're involved with in a month's time. Planning is different.

Our loosest time yet, maybe the most productive season

We'd met someone briefly in Colorado who, in talking about their early years in Thailand and Cambodia, mentioned he played tennis. My ears pricked up. People who mention tennis only usually do so if they can actually play. I contacted him in Bangkok, said we were coming out and could he put us in touch with people. Connections got made, people were informed, and somehow someone met us at the airport and took us to somewhere deep in the city.

The team back in Colorado were connected to, and supporting, several projects in the north of Thailand. One such small project being to set up an orphanage and school for the babies and young children of Burmese refugees, who having made it across the border, were detained indefinitely by the sometimes uncaring Thai Police.

This was the sort of spirited project that YWAM created wherever they went. See a need, meet a need. Now, anyone dedicated enough can make this last for a short season. Soon enough though, you need somewhere to do it, people to work with you, and money to make it last and keep it going. This would be where I came in. I'd help ensure that it was administered in such a way that it would be there in ten years' time if needed.

We made contact with them. And this is how it worked. Spend time, solve a problem, make progress, see the story get shared, get invited to help fix someone else's problem. Sometimes stay a while, and sometimes move somewhere new, depending upon the problem and location.

Creative accounting and home-schooling solutions

Every visitor to YWAM Bangkok is given a guide to the city, culture and customs. Mrs M was struggling with the heat, it was so very hot and humid. The boys and I decided we'd explore. They would do their classes online and on their laptops in the morning for an hour or two and then we'd jump on a bus, or train or taxi and head into the centre of Bangkok. I do sometimes shudder to recollect just how much freedom I gave them then. Jordan was just coming up to fifteen and Joel still only twelve. I'd sit in a café somewhere and tell them they've got a couple of hours to have a look around and then join me again. The boys got themselves haircuts, went shopping and exploring, bought food and drink and generally had a great time.

We'd then hop on a water taxi and visit a temple, or go and see the reclining Buddha, so some other such attraction. We had to work out whether offers of help were typical tourist scams or generally helpful locals. It felt sort of safe, but by now of course, the standards by which we were assessing risk were completely at odds with our British upbringing and culture!

Eating in restaurants was fun, the smaller the more enjoyable, and it mostly involved pointing at a picture of something we'd not tried before and seeing what it was.

Having "acclimatised" ourselves to Thailand, we then took a short internal flight to Chiang Rai in the north. There we were deposited into the guest quarters of a small community, which did have electricity and a ceiling fan. There were a few strange noise from the jungle outside our windows, which we later learned were from to-be-avoided-at-all-costs lizards, poisonous snakes and various other critters. The toilet was outside, in the dark and were the self-flush types.

You had to shake the room door before opening it, so the cockroaches and scorpions would not drop on you. We found a toad sitting on the girl's toilet, so every visit my wife made was proceeded by us shooing away any form of wildlife. The boys discovered that the big black scorpions didn't move very quickly. They then used sticks to play with their new pets. We told them they couldn't play with the local dogs so they made do.

My work started with helping the local community leader get his accounts up to date. He'd been using some US personal tax accounting software to try and manage a multi project, rather complex charity, or collection of charitable enterprises. I suggested that he ought to be using a proper accounting system, but they were so fearful of running out of money that they wouldn't purchase it. In the end, Mrs M and I paid for it, downloaded and installed it and then I spent the next couple of weeks entering several years of data so he could see the history.

This was a revelation for him, all of a sudden he could see, at a glance, all the different operations, could check budgets and plan cash flow. It was liberating. He was transformed. Instead of holding on to everything, scared it was all going to fall down, he was now releasing everyone to go and do what they wanted to do.

Now that was a productive couple of weeks.

My wife however, was struggling. Romantic notions of mine, not hers by the way, of exotic travel were trashed, when we learnt that the snakes were everywhere in the grass outside the windows. She needed civilisation and needed it now. Few English speakers, no Wi-Fi, community living on a more basic level, and lots of exotic dangerous animals, together with a continuation of the heavy bleeding she'd started to suffer in India. I made some calls, found a Bed & Breakfast (B&B) in Chiang Mai which was much more tourist friendly, but possibly for the wrong reasons, and then negotiated a discount as we'd be there for several weeks. With a rented car for the day, we moved to the B&B, which even had a small pool. They all loved it. There was Wi-Fi for the home-schooling and a/c in the room. I immediately returned to Chiang Rai and continued the work there, with an incentive to be as quick and efficient as possible, so I could re-join my family.

Back in Chiang-Mai, this time by bus. There are fifty nine letters and symbols in the Thai alphabet, so reading any of the signs was tough.

Prostitutes and ice-cream and common sense

We were introduced to someone else supported by the Colorado community, Emmi. Emmi ran a small café, using this as a way of employing ex-street girls and engaging them back into the community. It was however loss making and she didn't have a business brain. I got involved in marketing, product reviews, stocks, and creative income generation. They thought they needed to stock every single conceivable flavour of ice-cream despite only selling a scoop or two of some of them daily! For accountants, it would all be simple common sense.

Jordan was required to do a community work project each year for his home-school curriculum and elected to volunteer in the café for a couple of weeks.

I rented a motorcycle to get around, which was great fun. Emmi was happy by the time we had finished. It was fun in Thailand that a Honda Cub was deemed appropriate family transport, although I tried only ever to take one other passenger.

Another small charity project heard we were in town and asked if I could be of help to them also. This was, again, installing a simple accounting system and reviewing their previous few years transactions and then making sense of it all. I found them all sorts of cash they didn't know they had. Magic. They were very happy with me.

Business culture is still a culture to be learned

In helping one of the charities to get established properly, they needed to gain visa granting status for their overseas national workers. Another local agency, who had been there several years, with this visa approval already in place, said they'd help. So, we took them to lunch and I thought, with my functional hat on, and assuming that his time was valuable, went straight into the questions.

He immediately put his hand up and stopped me. "Tell me" he said, "Who are you, how should I do business with you unless I know who you are and where you come from"? It did stop me in my tracks, business here was so much more relational. Even the concept of gift-giving, which appears to a UK mind almost to be bribery, can then be seen in the context of working with friends, and friends give each other gifts.

It took a while, but our local contacts said that they'd come to learn that cash is used simply as a convenient means of exchanging/giving gifts. It's not a bribe as such, but enabled the gift to become whatever would truly be a blessing to the recipient. Our western (UK, European and US) business principles on bribery and gift giving, rather unhelpfully, has no interpretation for this other than "illegal". Our friends mentioned to their business contacts the problems that cash gifts would cause them back home and asked whether baskets of fruit and such like would work? They were told "of course". The gift is indeed an act of relationship, not a bribe.

Chiang Mai Tourism

Middle aged white men were everywhere. We realised that this particular tourist part of town is right in the middle of the entertainment that Thailand can be famous for. I'd pop out and buy groceries, spot some old white guy and make a judgement about what he was here for, and then realised that I was of course a middle aged white guy wandering around too! I took Jordan with me more often after that. Strange to think back on walking around the red light district with my fifteen year old son was a normal response.

We wanted to see a little more of the local, different, entertainment and sought out a Thai-Boxing venue. The first one was at the end of a chain of brothel bars, so we skipped past that and went to the next one. Well we did, but only after walking past several unseemly establishments and it gradually dawned on us where we were! Okay, this, Thai-Boxing, is a seriously entertaining way to spend an evening.

We were amongst very few westerners and felt almost local in joining in. Thai-Boxing is brutal, but at least nowadays they can wear padding downstairs and don't use cut glass in their gloves. They had a female match, which was tough to watch. There was then a drunken volunteer bout where several combatants were all put in a ring together, blindfolded and the winner the last one standing. Now that was a fun event.

Jordan turned fifteen whilst he was out there. Over the years we hadn't always been able to celebrate birthdays with friends. So we came up with the idea of "memory days", allowing them to choose to do something as a memory. This time Jordan chose bungee-jumping. To prepare himself for this he watched endless hours of YouTube clips, primarily of when it goes wrong. There was even a clip of the centre where we'd arranged to go, when someone had slipped out their harness on the way down. Encouraging, but he was determined. Although scared, he did it. I was a very proud dad that day.

The film Inception came out in Thailand whilst we were there and Jordan and I borrowed a car and went to the Cinema, which was on one end of the shopping centre. It was late, the film involving, and somehow, as we tried to find our way back to the car park, took a wrong turn. We went through a door into the shopping centre, by now empty and dark. What we should have done was to turn right around and back through the door, but that one-way door closed right behind us. To say it was surreal is an understatement, especially after watching Inception; the escalators didn't work, the only real lighting was coming through the roof from outside and it took a while to eventually find a door that opened through back into the parking area. Jordan held it together and for my part I kept a relaxed demeanour, but was also making contingency plans for how we'd sleep the night until the shops opened up the next morning.

Joel turned thirteen a couple of months later, there was a Micro-Light training centre a few hours out of town. Clubbing together his grand-parents gift money meant we could afford an hour's flight. He loved that. It was a bouncy, interesting flight, he later confessed that he was quite scared for most of the journey, especially the landing.

Burma and LOTR

We'd been intending of course to return to the USA one day and pick up, amongst other things, our work with the Burmese refugees.

The Thai tourist visas usually only last a short while and so many longer term visitors have to repeatedly exit the country and get their papers re-stamped. This, I imagine, helps the government keep tabs on foreigners, but it also means additional revenue from all the visas. The Thai/Burmese border town of Tachileik is therefore well geared towards inter-country services.

The boys and I decided, even though the visas we had didn't really require it, that we'd head to Burma for the day. As you do. We really wanted to be able to identify with our young Burmese friends for a start. It was a really unusual place to visit, not quite the tourist hotspot we imagined at all.

We were confronted with a choice immediately upon entering Burma, handing over your passport and receiving back a paper receipt for it. The choice is you don't enter Burma! As you return again, you collect your passport. All sorts of thoughts about how that could go wrong danced in front of me. But, "when in Rome" and everyone appeared happy with this arrangement. I felt nervous about it the whole time we there. As soon as we stepped over the threshold we were met by a street seller, with remarkably good English, keen to sell us all sorts of things, but with an almost unhealthy interest in who we were and why we were there. He said he'd learnt to speak English by watching John Wayne movies, and said his name was John. He was pleasant enough but I didn't want what he was selling. The next few street vendors were trying to push hash, coke, Viagra, paracetamol, a bizarre mix. We were followed by one old lady beggar who just wouldn't give up. I would have relented but her aggressive manor simply annoyed me! We bought a load of "genuine" DVDs. Well, all the DVDs we buy in the west are probably made in China anyway, and we were simply buying at source.

We strayed into a coffee place in the market, which could have been straight off the set of Lord of the Rings, as it was fitted out for Hobbits. Perfect size for the local Burmese, we just felt a little ridiculous. John reappeared at the next table. John also popped up again the next street we rounded.

We eventually found a larger restaurant with normal size plastic garden furniture and a menu where we could point at pictures of food. This was the last time we saw John, trying to hide behind a large newspaper a few tables away. We decided that "John" must have been a spy, or a secret agent or some kind of government agent. It sort of made our day.

A new country, a different culture

We had made friends with an American/South African couple and their family in Colorado. They had recently moved out to Penang in Malaysia and were connected to several local projects, all of which could do with qualified and competent financial assistance.

We hopped onto a flight out from Chiang Mai and across into Kuala-Lumpur and from there on to the jewel of the orient, Penang. Pollution and over-crowing plus severe construction mismanagement means that the "jewel" title doesn't really apply anymore. The sea had become toxic, and nobody did scuba anymore. Where we lived was still part of the old British part of town and looked like it. Elsewhere, it was downtown, original and run down – suitable therefore for UNESCO heritage status - or high rise block after high rise block and dusty and dirty.

Care in the community wasn't a core tenant of life in this part of the world. Whether this is due to the local expression of Islam or a unique Malaysian culture is hard to say. I am aware also that for this episode I am looking through a different set of glasses, so forgive any offence. Our friends were connected to a homeless shelter, and a feeding program for the dispossessed. To be Malaysian is to be Muslim, in fact ID cards start with your religion first. Chinese and Indian ethnic people are not bothered about, as they don't really count as citizens, so we were informed by locals. They pay higher rates of tax for example and can't attend schools or obtain public services in the same way either. The food programme would be visited by the Religious Police daily during Ramadan and the programme shut down if a single Malay homeless person was seen to have been given food or water.

A friend of theirs had chosen to change his faith. He then had his mind changed back again with the helpful use of a battery being wired up to a tender part of his anatomy. So this was a strange culture to be in for sure.

They also undertook advocacy work for indentured, primarily Indian and Burmese workers, who were often severely mistreated locally. Prisons and courts were all conducted in Malay, with no access to interpretation services, save for the ones our friends group provided.

My professional work was simply to assess the way their books were being done. They used an unfamiliar, Australian based accounting system which was prepared by using an external firm of accountants locally. However, they didn't know what to ask, what reports or information could be available, nor how to set budgets in this context. I walked them through all the questions and possibilities and helped them start a new era of open communication with the accountants. Again, I think, a success.

Having time on my hands, I also then arranged all the practical details for their upcoming office move and re-structure. Like you do.

Contraband available

"Hello my friend, are you British? I have something special for you." The local shop-keeper, of Chinese descent, approached me. What on earth did he mean I thought? Was this drugs, or alcohol? He took me round the maze of corridors and add-ons and sheds and buildings that formed his "shop". We eventually stopped by a freezer, and furtively looking around to make sure nobody was looking, pulled out some sausages. "I have bacon too if you wish?!"

This was so tempting. However, we were in a block of flats, and I knew only too well that the smell of fried bacon would have set some alarm bells off! It's not an easy smell to disguise.

Help always close by

It was a public holiday and so Jordan and I decided to take the antique, as old as me, Honda Cub. It was our family transport for this short season. We navigated our way to and then across the massive bridge that separated Penang from the mainland. The Cub in question was borrowed from someone locally and I had already had new pistons and new brakes put on, which cost me about a tenner from a local chap working from under a tree, to make it less unsafe. We could squeeze three of us on it at a pinch, but not all four.

The bridge was about twenty km away, but with it being a public holiday, there was almost no traffic and we made it quickly. Several hundred meters across, the bike started to weave and buck horribly. With my precious son on the back, and the poisonous jelly fish infested waters a few feet, but a long drop away, I gratefully wrestled the bike to a stop. Now what? I imagined the long walk back with a broken bike, in the heat, with no shops open nor help available. Making sure Jordan was okay, and explaining that this would one day make for a great story, we needed to get ready for a long walk.

Just at that moment, an Indian chap rode by and stopped. In sign language we displayed our puncture and he grabbed his toolkit. For the princely sum of $8 (including generous tip) we had a repaired inner tube and we were on our way. Thankful for a kind stranger we were chuffed to bits at our good fortune.

We continued across the long road bridge and entered the mainland and stopped at a roadside café for drinks and snacks. This was almost like a different country. We decided that maybe we'd had enough adventure for one day and turned around, eager to share our story with Mum, Joel and our friends.

They casually mentioned that there was a recent spate of so called mechanics throwing tacks across carriageways of major roads so they could arrive and repair punctures. A neat little business model.

Western world wonders

Another contact in Australia said that they needed help with an international anti-malaria project, and so that too became part of the trip. This felt like I'd be making a tangible difference to a project on an entirely different scale. "Buzzoff" was working towards completely eradicating malaria, starting in East Timor. When we put our trip together back in the spring, extending flights didn't add too much to the costs, as it was all in the general direction of some routine round the world flight packages.

We arrived in Melbourne and were picked up by someone from the local YWAM base. They then explained that the malaria project contact had been detained in Asia somewhere and wasn't expected for several weeks.

I mentioned that I was here to help with finances and budget setting and accounting, but they said they had it all covered. Thanks very much though.

So, this was different. Melbourne was cold. We'd gone across Asia and things had become more and more bizarre, frankly. We now took this final flight and ended up in what seemed to be Kent (England). The names of the roads were familiar places, houses and streets looked familiar, even plants and gardens were the same. Plus, it was painfully cold. We'd spent several months living on an Asian budget; street meals were less than $1 and accommodation cheap, and clothing sort of optional, more for discretion than warmth.

Australia was expensive, really expensive. We went shopping for some warm clothes. I came back with a cheap tracksuit top and fleeces for the boys and that took a couple of week's spending money. Fortunately, they were deemed worthy recipients of the City's foodbank programme. Everyone in YWAM community contributes in some way to the running of their own project/base as there are no paid staff for anything. My assigned tasks were to help with the foodbank collection, storage and distribution and supervise the dustbin collections and waste management. Humbling. My entire career had culminated into being Director of Dustbins for some bunch of strangers the other side of the world. It was a long way from Kansas, it was also very cold.

Eventually, they invited me into the office when one of their external accounting volunteers was sick, as they needed help inputting some transactions. I started to ask a couple of questions about their reporting and budget setting and that sort of thing. By the time we departed Oz a few weeks later, they were asking if I could stay longer to help! I think I made a small difference, but it's hard to say really.

What was good was the opportunity for us as a family to spend time together, to rest and to assess what we would be doing next. We'd been living out of suitcases for nearly three years now, sometimes staying in places for a few days, sometimes weeks and occasionally months. We met my uncle, who I'd not seen for over thirty years, who went off on a gap year, got as far as Melbourne and stayed put.

The perks of this life season included a week's trip up the Gold Coast to the town of 1770 (Seventeen Seventy), where Cook apparently "discovered" Australia. It's funny this "discovery" thing. In Colorado Springs, there is a brilliant place called "Garden of the Gods" which was "discovered" by some American, who was probably European. Never mind the fact that the Native American tribes had been using it as a winter retreat for thousands of years before that.

Mrs M's health was deteriorating, and so we cut short our plans and headed back to the UK. We honestly now didn't know what we'd do or where we'd go. We arrived back in the UK, unsure whether this was indeed "home" anymore, just before Christmas.

Her dad would of course have us to stay again, although it was now Mr and Mrs, after his April Marriage. It was also a small flat, and not entirely suitable for a family of four to inhabit with the newlyweds.

We mentioned our housing dilemma to other longstanding friends, who themselves had travelled much of the world. They thought an old South African friend of theirs was living in Switzerland and recalled him having mentioned something about an empty property? Anyway, a quick email elicited an immediate and a favourable reply. "Of course you can come, we do have spare property, in fact we have several, and if you can help our charity part time, then that would be your contribution".

Somehow, without trying, friendships and service to those in need was yielding yet more results. There was no way we could have engineered or even imagined this in our wildest dreams. Living in Switzerland had been one of those life dreams for me, and I'd given it up when I left Roche for the world of penniless volunteering!

Investment in friendships brings its own reward

Water the gardens of others

Switzerland, land of milk and honey

After eight months living out of suitcases, we arrived in Switzerland.

Our home would be a detached Swiss cottage, in a hamlet, eight km up the mountains, with views of Lake Geneva and Mont Blanc. Not at all shabby.

The Swiss do things well, very well indeed.

We were welcomed, work permits were obtained, housing arranged, connections made. A neighbour shared their WI-FI with us for free.

Community in a Swiss context is done on an entirely different scale. In this little Swiss village, several residents in our immediate block shared a common washing machine and each one assigned a different day. Someone must have, at some time, originally bought the washer and dryer? The heating for most of the village came from a shared "chauffage" a communal heating furnace. In fact the village itself owned acres of forest, they then took it in turns to cut and store wood, and the wood somehow made its way into a furnace that sent the heat, under the road, up and into our house.

We did have an open fire as well, with wood which we were welcome to help ourselves to, but this was really just for visual affect.

We had somewhere to live. Mrs M had a home, a nice cottage, a brand new kitchen, open fire, a pretty garden and nice neighbours who would go above and beyond to be helpful. The boys even had a proper classroom – the unused second floor conservatory. This was indeed luxury, especially as for most of the time in Thailand they were sitting on plastic garden chairs outside a friendly neighbour's garage, hiding from the sun but trying to jump onto his Wi-Fi signal.

For my part, I agreed to spend half the week in their finance office.

I know "accounting" (Neo, the Matrix)

The community base here was a former large orphanage with its own farm and was now a training centre for international child development, and agricultural training, in the wider French speaking world.

The accounts were fairly simple, and even if in French and German, understandable. Years of accounting packages meant you instinctively know what something is depending on where it sits in the Chart of Accounts (COA) or Trial balance (TB).

The hardest thing to explain to them was how bad debt provisions worked, even to perfectly fluent multi lingual Swiss. That's when you realise that actually, accounting is in fact its own language too.

We had by now been living as voluntary workers for nearly four years. Our time in Jamaica was another two. We'd made mistakes and had accidental successes in this arena. So, someone else, connected to a friend of a friend, suggested I present to a network of marketing and communication voluntary workers, who were all meeting in Jordan a few weeks later.

I was excited at the opportunity of travel again, and to somewhere I knew nothing of. I knew little of the culture and customs, not even how being British would be perceived. I did know that the King of Jordan attended school in the UK, had military training at Sandhurst, even serving in the British military, so he must like the British.

Presentation is crucial, NGO Advice

I had read an article (Nepali Times 8/11/14) that asked interviewers to rate candidates on their first impressions only, literally as they walked through the door and said "hello". Separately and later, the same candidates' CVs (resumes) were reviewed by the interviewers, requiring them to pick out the best ones to take forward. There was an amazing 80% correlation.

I'd somehow been invited to Jordan to attend an international volunteer agency's annual communication conference, primarily to deliver a few short presentations on living as a volunteer worker. Being sat next to a Doctor on the plane it really struck me that I wasn't clear as to who I was and what I was doing, at least on a presentational basis. I was a Christian going into a Muslim country to talk to mainly other Christians about sustaining long term works as voluntary workers. I felt confused and a little awkward.

I determined to resolve this incongruence and started to think about who I was, what I was doing, what service did I provide; living near Geneva and all these world renowned charities really helped this process.

I investigated NGO accounting, administration, consultancy, whatever was left as an unregistered domain name basically! I discovered NGO Advice (www.ngoadvice.com). This then would be "me" to the outside world, my representation. It fitted. There was actually a dearth of Accountants prepared to work for nothing. I'd met very few on my travels, which was why what I did was so valuable.

In reality I was starting to discover, at the same time as a few others, there were other socially minded Accountants that were coming together. I joined MANGO, not the Ladies Wear company, but Management Accounting for NGOs. My interview with them was to prove to their satisfaction my skills, experience of "field" accounting and discuss my motivation. One of their senior team was bi-lingual and so a section of the interview was in French; amazingly I remembered enough to scrape through the "I speak French" bit of my CV. They work with charities and NGOs to provide basic training and to help recruit quality field staff to primarily the most unglamorous development situations.

Subsequently I also came across A.F.I.D., Accounting for International Development, which exists to enable Accountants to use their skills in a development context during holidays and short career breaks. They do charge you for the service though, after all they are still Accountants and I guess their volunteers are usually all well paid Accountants looking for a quick development and charity fix!

Professionalising my CV

This then was my CV's salvation, finally a way of redeeming six years of professional wanderings. I stumbled across LinkedIn © and, seeing how this was now being used, updated that part of my presentation too. For a season, especially the next couple of years, it seemed that in almost every business encounter, I would be researched ahead of time. At last, my experiences and achievements could be brought together in a coherent and acceptable way, almost fluid and meaningful, almost like a properly thought-out career plan!

NGO Advice has morphed into Meggs Management Ltd. I retain the domain name, one never knows who might want to buy it one day.

There are several people named Meggs around the world, just look up LinkedIn, who are much more successful than I am!

Mayfair in London with Joule Africa

We'd been in Switzerland seven months. Whilst I spoke French, and the boys' friends all spoke English, Mrs M was not confident enough to start learning. It became increasingly isolating for her.

Even a simple trip to the doctors meant she had to steel herself to try and explain quite nuanced concepts. Despite the typical medical professional's high quality grasp of English, it never felt quite right.

Relationship tip; keep a watch out for this if you travel as a family

She'd had enough. The ill-health that had dogged her since India was still there. She decided that we'd return to the UK forthwith. We had nowhere to go, but this wasn't now her problem. We had friends in the UK she would stay with for a few days and I packed her off on the plane, ready to follow with the boys and all our stuff, later. Our amazing friends, Ian and Nicky, gave her a front door key and said we were never even to say we were coming, their home was our home. We still have their key to this day. Now that's what I call friendship.

I didn't know what to do. Thanks goodness for the internet though. An inspired thought popped up. What about researching Christian holiday accommodation? Surely, with our recent "Christian service" credentials, we might be able to obtain a cheap week or so just to get us back in the country without being a burden on anybody?

I found somewhere online, that I misread as Eastbourne, but was in fact "Easebourne house". I quickly and desperately sent off an email, to see if they had a spare week. They replied that they were closed for the season as they were intending to sell the property and purchase a new one in Cornwall. They finished the email off with the following - "But if you wanted to, and promised to leave when we need you to, you could always stay for a few weeks whilst we get the property onto the market, just give us a donation".

I then realised my mistake in reading the name, but the house was only located about an hour away from where we used to live in Eastbourne. The holiday home was in fact a four bedroomed detached house in a hugely expensive village in West Sussex. Somehow, we had managed to land on our feet, again. The neighbours were nice too. They lived in a rather pleasant, large, country manor house, with their own floodlit tennis court, which was unused and at the boy's disposal. We had bridle paths outside our gate, and now space and time to work out what we were going to do next.

If it wasn't all true and you simply read about this in some sort of novel, you might scarcely believe it. However, within a week of moving back to the UK we had a new home and space in which to unpack all the various boxes of stuff we'd deposited in various friend's garages and lofts. We unpacked and hid away the suitcases.

It was turning out that we didn't actually need our own home, it appeared as though every time we needed one, one would present itself.

Some coincidences you simply couldn't make up

It had always been a tough ask, being a qualified accountant and living off the donations and kindness of others. Don't get me wrong, many people, far more than you might realise, are more than willing and even want to support people "out there" making a difference in the world. What we found though, was that the least qualified had the easiest job in asking for support. Professional people we came across all agreed that the more qualified you are, the more people expect you to get a "proper job"!

Of course, in my mind, I did have a proper job, just one that most accountants would never do, because the pay was so pants. They didn't do all that studying in order to be poor.

Within a couple of weeks most of our support stopped. Being back in the UK, everyone expected, albeit subconsciously maybe, that I'd get paid work. I didn't want to do that. I already had a job, it just didn't pay me anything!

Accountants aren't perceived as voluntary workers

For context, our annual family income, including one off gifts, gift aid and so on, was around £15,000. It came via monthly cheques and standing orders that varied from £5 to £100. It came from people we knew and loved, and from some who we had never met but who wanted to contribute to the work we were engaged with. Somehow we travelled the world, lived, ate, schooled the boys, drove cars and managed a household. I'd never been so well off earning so little.

From rags to riches – it still happens

I'd met a chap once in Colorado a few years back and we'd discussed accounting and finances in a development context. The chat was maybe twenty minutes, and I hadn't met him since. Somehow, coincidentally, I'd ended up playing five-a-side with his son-in-law somewhere though.

I took a call on my mobile one afternoon. It was Lynn, describing a start-up venture that his son was a partner in, that they were having trouble finding quality and trustworthy accounting support, and that he thought I'd be ideal.

Again, given our dire financial situation, a wonderful coincidence.

I found myself in Mayfair a couple of days later, with a suit I'd worn once in the past five years, in front of a couple of people whose shirts cost more than my suit. They described in detail the multi-billion dollar project to build a hydro-electric dam in Sierra Leone. Could I help them to get their fledgling finances in order?

I told them that I wasn't really interested in a long term role and that I worked as a volunteer, but seeing as their project fitted in nicely with my development focus, I'd help them for a few months. They asked me what fees I'd like, and barely hid their smiles when I suggested an obviously low ball figure, saying they'd have a think and get back to me. I wasn't entirely sure I was what they were looking for, I didn't fit what I imagined was their ideal candidate profile!

They called me back that evening, and offered me at least a third more than I'd asked for and asked me when could I start?

I'd gone from rags to riches, literally. In the US we were getting clothes from the equivalent of a free charity shop, run alongside a foodbank. I was now working in Mayfair amongst the richest people in the country and it was I confess a weird feeling.

I could do the work though. Accounting principles remain the same. I did have a unique gift though, of which I was not yet fully conscious, that meant I was superbly qualified to help this potentially billion dollar company.

Relationships, again, still, always, important

Who needs a house when you have access to homes?

We'd come across another voluntary worker, from India, who mentioned they were staying in some specialised housing. I got the contact details and made an enquiry. Harpenden, Herts, some of the most expensive post codes in the country. There was, a few year back, a local business gentleman who really valued "overseas missions" but felt unable to go. Instead he bought some land and paid for several houses and flats to be built. The houses were for returning missionaries and voluntary workers on furlough, or home rest, and the flats were for retired missionaries who had nowhere to live, as they'd dedicated their lives to serving others. He'd then handed the management of these to Pilgrim's Friend, a charity specialising in elderly residential care.

I explained our situation. Somehow we fitted their requirements, they had a house becoming available and we could move in a couple of months' time. So we packed up our boxes and moved up to an area I'd scarcely have afforded even when I was on the career ladder. We could stay for up to a year and in the end remained there eighteen months, until we decided a return to Eastbourne was our next step.

Malawi visits and lectures and accounting consultancy

Meanwhile, I had an already planned trip to Malawi. I'd been in Mayfair for two months, moved house again, and was due to fly to Blantyre literally the day after moving.

Friends of ours who had moved to Malawi had kick-started an old charitable enterprise. Old fashioned Gospel preaching for sure, but this was set alongside medical training, food relief and orphanage support work. This was a solid attempt to minister to the entire person! Those working in such poor countries are never able to afford quality training nor international visitors and years earlier I'd promised them that I would volunteer my time, and at my expense, fly out and help them however I could. It was a promise I was determined to keep, especially now.

Jordan joined me, and at sixteen he was up for another little adventure. I was asked to help look at their finances but also to help deliver a week's training to around twenty volunteers and potential staff. They would need help understanding what they were about to do, the values that underpinned this lifestyle, how to exist as unpaid workers and so on. We'd made enough mistakes during our now seven years of living this way, all I had to do was tell them what we did, and suggest that they do the opposite!

Jordan was asked to go and help with maintenance work at a "nearby" orphanage. It involved a three bus two hour journey to get there and a full on day working in the African sun. He did it all without complaining. I think he was still in the mode of thinking that the worse it got the better it would be! His companion, guide and work colleague was a bundle of energy called Charles.

Charles relayed to Jordan the story of how, once he had discovered "faith", he had wanted to right as many of the wrongs in his life he could. Like many others locally, he had bribed his way to a driving licence, rather than learn and take the test. One day he felt compelled to go to the Police and confess this to someone in charge and was fully prepared to be imprisoned for it. The local Police Chief was so impressed he let him off and so a great local working relationship was forged, and one that's not always there.

Daniel has sought out the Police, deliberately making relationship with them and always stopping by thanking them for all their hard work – he says that he's speaking over them the sort of Police he wants them to be! These relationships have yielded positive outcomes in all sorts of ways with the work they do and the protection of their families.

I attempted to help with the finances. Locally, like many places in Africa, cash is king. There are no receipts, and whoever is in charge really has to manage everything directly. I helped him with a move to an App on his phone to help, but "accounting" it was not.

We were invited to go out into the bush with a small team and show the Jesus film in the local Chichewa language. It's amazing, you drive for hours, down into the Shiree value, spelt "shire". I truly believe it was a quaint Victorian English attempt at naming a place after home, which then got mixed up in local pronunciation over many years.

It was over fifty Celsius and we were camping. However, being the honoured guests on the trip, at least we slept in the roof tent on top of the Toyota. We removed the panels, kept the mosquito mesh in place and had the most amazing night sky as our back-drop. Extreme poverty meant no electricity and therefore zero light pollution. Climbing to the top of the nearest hill still elicited not a single sign of civilisation so far as we could see. We did signs of life early in the morning though, as our truck was surrounded by dozens of children eager to catch a glimpse of whoever was sleeping in the roof-tent!

They show the film, people come, they share a story of how Jesus is a blessing and then connect the people with the nearest church. These local pastors are also given medical training, as most people have no access to medical services, and people's lives are improved.

A strange "working week". Accounting does not have to be boring.

To keep the costs down, and in truth, to go for an authentic African experience with Jordan, we flew into Lilongwe and then made our way from Lilongwe to Blantyre by bus. Sounds so simple in hindsight. Our hosts had made a connection with other contacts in Lilongwe to collect us from the airport and take us to the bus station downtown. Our "taxi" was by a country mile the worst car I have ever sat in. The seat was disconnected to the floor due to the rust, it had to be bump started every time, and the clutch was so weak it felt like we ought to peddle like the Flintstones. It broke down on the way, several times. We were requested to pay for their repairs as we left them beside the road, after spending an hour or two attempting to pour water into the radiator whilst it leaked straight out. One definition of insanity is repeating the same task, getting the same outcome, but repeating it again hoping that something different might happen? A passing official taxi took us to the bus station and we somehow found the bus that would take us to Blantyre. This was not at all easy, as none of the buses looked different and few had signs indicating the direction of travel. We settled in amongst the people, livestock, and luggage for a long ride. Not the most relaxing of experiences. Daniel met us at around one in the morning, semi naked as he'd given way most of his clothes away to a homeless person whilst waiting for us at the bus station. Quite a start to Africa on a budget!

Jordan and I bravely decided that we'd find the cash and fly back to Lilongwe for the return trip home. Arriving at Blantyre airport, we found it to be strangely quiet. Asking someone at the gate when the Air Malawi flight would arrive we were met with a startled look and told "Don't you know Air Malawi is grounded?" It had been deemed an unsafe airline, and had, apparently, been on the UN unsafe airline list for a while already.

I turned to Jordan and said that this would make a great story one day. Our learning opportunity for the day would be to realise we couldn't change anything and only had control of our reactions to these events. A call back to Daniel confirmed that even if Daniel would bring his car back immediately, there was no way we'd make the drive up in time.

I casually asked someone in a uniform behind a desk if there were any other flights due that day, to which he replied "one" which would leave in an hour or so. "Were there any seats left?" I tentatively enquired and he replied that there were just two, "would you like them?" This all seemed too good to be true and of course I wanted them! The only caveat being that I needed to pay by cash as there were no credit card facilities, and I didn't have any money on me. I said that my friend Daniel lived in Blantyre and what about if he came along that afternoon and paid for them later? To my astonishment he looked me up and down and said "sure"! He printed me off a receipt for the tickets. We were still a little anxious as we boarded the plane, especially when the security team came on board and dragged off another guest, apparently she didn't have the right ticket. We made our Lilongwe flight with just a few minutes to spare. There's a phrase often heard in those parts; "TIA". This is Africa.

I don't imagine being able to get away with that at Gatwick!

These aren't the droids you're looking for

On a future trip, this time with Joel, as we tried to get through Immigration they insisted everyone show their Yellow Fever certificates. In checking before we flew, this requirement didn't appear on the FCO site I might add. I routinely travel with mine, just in case. Joel didn't have one and the guard refused to allow him through into the terminal, not even off the runway. I was startled for a moment, but remembered Daniel's advice about Malawi/Africa. One must never, ever, admit to there being a problem, because problems need money or officialdom to resolve.

Somehow in my mind I recalled Star Wars and the Jedi mind trick, I waved my hand and said there wasn't a problem, I'd get it resolved once we were through. He raised his voice and repeated that we were not allowed into the country. I waved my hand again and repeated the fact that there was not a problem and he should just let us through. I looked at Joel, he knew what I was doing and smiled. We were waved through, I know not how. Joel likes this story.

I genuinely think that Africa, if you allow yourself to be open to it, is capable of delivering experiences and stories you couldn't make up.

A new season a new culture, Mayfair

We flew back and I was at my desk in Mayfair the following morning. My boss, one of the founders, then approached me, saying he'd been able to sleep peacefully for the first time in weeks, since my arrival. Would I consider joining them properly, as an employee?

Our support was still dwindling. There was no choice, so I said "of course, yes". They promptly increased my pay again. I'm fond of Andrew & Mark!

The company had employed a high flying South African accountant to be the FD in Sierra Leone, I would look after treasury for the group from London as well as the UK Company accounting. He though, was asking a lot of questions and appeared not to be enjoying himself. Being paid substantially more than me, I assumed because he was a specialist high flyer with international experience. I also assumed he was my superior. It was decided I'd go out and cover for him for a couple of weeks, whilst he was out of the country.

Unfortunately for Jessa, his experience at large American banking institutions and corporations meant that he'd never had to handle real business money. Sierra Leone, the sixth poorest nation on the planet, was a cash society. The underpinning of any large company is how you manage the small stuff. Of course, my special gifting was that as an unpaid voluntary worker with multiple small charities in different countries and cultures, I had seen how to manage cash. He was managing, in great detail, every item of expense on a personal excel sheet. Hugely detailed, unimaginably stressful in my opinion.

I spent the next two weeks setting up the processes and controls, and enabling the accounting system and local team to function.

Toyota Land-Cruisers and Drivers

One difference between multi-national companies, as well as larger NGOs, and the smaller charitable organisations, is how you get around town.

Our company had bought four brand new Toyota 4x4s and hired four drivers. This was what was expected of them by the Government. Most local NGOs did similar things and would be driven from place to place, hardly ever connecting with the very people they were there, on the face of it, to serve. It does make one wonder what lies behind their motivation. Is it just a career move, and the people they are serving a means to an end? Are the people real to them even?

What's your own attitude to risk? Are you happy with that answer?

Smaller charities, on the other hand, tend to go in and serve people where they're at. So, when I visited Freetown, I'd use the 4x4 to get into the office, which I was required to. But evenings and weekends were my time. I decided to walk up the hill, and came across a run-down beat-up tennis club perched on top. Chatting with a local guy, who was coaching the children, I discovered a retired army sergeant who was a former national champion back in the day. He told me this "Hilltop Club" used to have hundreds of European members, famously including Graham Greene, who wrote one of his books "The heart of the matter" from there, overlooking the bay below! I got his number and would call him for a game of tennis every time I came into town. This was a Freetown worth spending time in.

Continuing our life's theme of fully engaging and enjoying everyplace we lived, I wanted to see if anyone went scuba diving here. There was one choice, "the Greek guy" who lived on an offshore island, only accessible by fishing boat, typically outrigger canoe, who had such a business. Apparently the only scuba choice in the country. Several phone calls later and I drove up the coast to find him.

I'd got a map of the surrounding area. Unfortunately it was created about ten or twenty years ago, before the civil war and before nature had reclaimed the roads along the coast and through the jungle.

The drive up the so called road was interesting, well, challenging. It had rained, and over the years, the bush had reclaimed the original tarmac and concrete. This is actually the road pictured on the front cover of the book. What was left was a brown track, soft, boggy, slimy and of varying depths. Sometimes the car went forwards, but frequently sideways, as it slithered and slid making gradual progress. Either supreme confidence or utter ignorance meant I knew it wouldn't defeat me. However, deferring to my wife's clearly articulated instructions these days, I no longer say "what's the worst that could happen".

The village out of which the fishing boat would collect me had a rope toll. I paid the tiny toll and enquired if I could park my car, a $40,000 Toyota 4x4, for the week-end. I was told that I could pay a donation to the local boys club and they'd look after it for me. He seemed trustworthy and sincere and so I agreed to pay him $10 for the service. Looking back now, after a few years back in the UK, I sometimes wonder about my decisions and choices! They all appeared entirely rationale at the time. After another few phone calls I paid a fisherman to take me across in his boat and I was at "Banana Island".

I have come to realise that as much as I love the water, nearly all of my near death / close shave experiences have been on or in or around water. I was miles away from anywhere civilised, on a remote island, with no insurance cover that mattered, intermittent cell phone coverage, doing a dangerous sport with the "Greek guy". I decided that I'd be cautious and not dive any deeper than ten metres. Well cautious was a relative term, given all the previous observations!

I paid for the most expensive accommodation option, $15 a night including mosquito net. One could camp on the beach for $5 if you were tight for cash. Meals were taken communally, cooked by the host and his Sierra Leone wife. The highlight was then sitting in the large tree-house platform he had built whilst the dozen or so guests chatted the evening away as the sun set across the ocean, just a few feet below. He had a knackered old compressor, run by an equally knackered diesel generator, with which to get air in the tanks. As he was using the same air as we were, I assumed it all to be safe. I briefly flashed my PADI card but insisted on taking it easy and only doing a gentle reef dive. I love diving, this was brilliant, and a perfect antidote to the craziness of Freetown and setting up accounting systems for a fledgling Hydro Electric corporation. I stayed just the one night and returned back to my safe, and washed, Toyota and headed back to town.

I went back a few more times, each time to review and sharpen up the finances and processes. The project however, was perpetually being stalled at a government level. Some elements of foul play were surely at work. An average English village has more access to electricity than the entire nation of Sierra Leone. It hardly seemed possible that the government would delay something this potentially beneficial to the people of their country.

Our offices were next to the various ministry buildings and therefore in the best part of the capital city. There was mostly no electricity other than our generator. There was no water, except that brought up to our fifth floor offices by the boys who would fetch up plastic containers. Toilet flushing was by hand. Even the bagged water couldn't be trusted. I typically travel with an ultra violet (UV) "Steripen" to properly purify drinking water, and rarely get sick travelling. In Sierra Leone, I was sick every visit. It didn't matter what I did to try and stay healthy, it got me sooner or later.

Back in London, another project was awarded, this time in Cameroon. My French would come in useful once again and so I did another accounting audit visit to assess the reporting and systems. This time I was just there to help embed the reporting and reconciliations. Once again, cash was king, although Cameroon is a very different, and wealthier, country to Sierra Leone. We were told by someone close to the Minister of Energy that he wanted to award us the contract, they were fed up with a fresh colonial invasion, this time by the Chinese. The Chinese had their hands all over this and many other African countries, securing the long term supplies of raw materials. Clever and forward thinking, but by now, not always universally welcomed at a local government level.

We bought a brand new Land-Rover Defender, a white painted "Africanised" model. Our local and Government appointed liaison helped us find a driver. The local manager suggested, but didn't insist upon, training. While I was there the driver told me there was nothing the 4WD training specialists could teach him about driving anyway. A week or so after I returned to the UK, we were sent pictures of the Defender, on its side, with the roof and sides collapsed, after being rolled. The road was deserted, flat and nobody else was involved. Young men insisting that they know everything is, apparently, a universal truth in all cultures.

Back in Freetown again, a local Chinese company was enquiring about the potential contracts that would arise for a large scale Hydro project. We were invited around one evening, firstly to play Basketball, then to dinner. Apart from the communal living, my memory of that night revolves around their apparent favourite night time game of drinking rice whisky competitively. A rare hangover for me followed, as I went head to head with their Financial Controller.

In Sierra Leone, they had ripped up the old train lines to lay new tracks, and were transporting raw materials out of mines to Chinese ships in Chinese built ports. One of the driver's comments seemed to sum up the prevailing attitude to this fresh colonial invasion "I can give my family breakfast tomorrow".

My driver also gave me another insight into the local thinking. One day I hesitantly raised the subject of the civil war and the reputation for child soldiers. Having finally plucked up enough courage to watch Blood Diamond, sights in the film were by now familiar to me. He calmly informed me that his eldest son had been taken a year before fighting stopped and was transformed into a child soldier. Some ten years on and they are still dealing with the aftermath of this in their family; it's personal, not just an item on the BBC. He then said that everyone in the local community knew who the perpetrators were, but had decided not to live in bitterness, and so forgiving without forgetting was what they chose to do. For the future and for their children's sake. The Sierra Leonean people are absolutely amazing.

Never be too proud to accept instruction, even when you are expert

I continued visiting Malawi, and ended up visiting and working there four times. The last time, as the local community building projects took shape, we started to make progress on the accounting too.

My friend Daniel, after a week spent teaching new voluntary workers and a few days helping with the charity's accounting, suggested a couple of nights away by Lake Malawi. I figured that after a number of these trips, I was due some R&R! He packed the dinghy, and I had confidence in him as after all he'd spent a couple of years as a sailing instructor in the south of France. The afternoon found me on an antique weathered Laser, my only previous experience nearly drowning off the Isle of Wight, Daniel and family in their motorboat. I was already nervous about the organ burrowing snail parasites called bilharzia, which you basically get just by coming into contact with the water. Nearing shore after rounding the headland, after a good hour or so, I noticed some small hippos off to my right and sailed passed them to the shore. Looking back we saw they were babies and mum was just nearby. We had to get back, as we only had jungle between us and our cottage and it was nearing dusk. A lady emerged warning us loudly about the Hippos, suggesting we head back into the water but in the opposite direction, "but that's where the crocodiles are". "I'd worry less about the crocs than mummy hippo though" she said comfortingly. No breeze and therefore a flappy sail meant some tense moments when we put out from the beach! Fortunately I saw no crocodiles and the hippos stayed their distance.

As we returned to the civilisation of Blantyre, we took a family trip to the pharmacy to collect anti-bilharzia medicine. It's almost a given that if you spend time near the lake, you'll catch it. Daniel and the family had long since given up the cheaper local medical offering, now preferring the more expensive but effective official solution. In the UK, I asked my own Doctor whether he thought I should take it, he said not to. A week later, I had a text from Daniel to say that his young son was peeing blood, and was just double checking to ensure I'd taken my medicine? I promptly took the tablets and waited. The severe reaction I displayed was, apparently, proof that the medicine was working and dealing with the little critters starting to take up residence. The "cure" was bad, but nothing compared to the long term effects of the potential parasitic infestation!

I finally did get a gun shoved in my face. Driving past a military parade, we were struck by how impressive it was. By the time we slowed down and I'd taken my camera out, there were two soldiers running at us with guns out. One pointed his gun in my face and the other grabbed the camera. We continued with "these aren't the droids" calm tones and finally, after an intervention by the commanding officer, received the camera back with a warning.

Back in the Mayfair offices, the money ran out. Large hydro projects take time and lots of cash and the Government was stalling.

Accounting principles are universal

Return to Eastbourne

Mrs M and I decided that we would remain in the UK now, and for this next season we would provide a stable platform for our boys to finish school and start University. Eastbourne was the closest place to home, we had lived there before, the boys were born in the local hospital and we had some amazingly faithful friends nearby.

We found a run-down farmhouse within our price bracket, cheap, as it had no heating we'd later discover. It had an antique, barely working Aga, open fireplace and sat in an acre of garden, in the corner of a reclaimed field, some five miles out of Eastbourne. We still cannot work out where the water come from, there being no water bills, as the garden well doesn't look up to the job. There are no neighbours, streetlights nor obvious signs of civilisation. Bliss.

As I write this now, sitting looking out across the gardens and farm of our temporary rental home, this is actually the longest we've been in a single location for twenty five years.

We're all in this together

I arrived back in work the day after signing a one year lease and was informed there was no more money coming in and would I sacrifice my salary for six months please? We were all in this together and we all needed to do our bit.

We were not, however, all truly equal in this regard, especially as my salary was on an entirely different scale! To their credit, the owners and CEO and COO were true to their word and would forgo their salaries for the next several months. My own circumstances were such that this wasn't an option open to me. I had no savings, no investments, no home and nothing worth more than a second hand bicycle!

One of my other colleagues was also an investor and had several million in the bank. Whilst being able to afford not to be paid, he would insist on a salary so others around him would take his input more seriously. Value is assigned to what one pays for, free advice is not always valued of course.

He was an entrepreneur that had built and twice now sold companies to US Investors and now wanted to put something of value back into society. Amongst his many unique qualifications was being a business mentor to the first ever winner of the UK talent show "The Apprentice". He'd been planning on doing a two year VSO assignment when he happened across Joule Africa and saw an opportunity to first invest monetarily in something of long-term "real" value and then to bring in his own considerable experience.

He recounted a story from one evening in Cameroon, where a visiting executive found themselves in the company of an attractive woman. Amazingly, this visitor thought he noticed an associate of their Government appointed contact for the project. He stopped everything. He was well on his way into a honey trap the like of Tom Cruise's character in The Firm. Impressively, he knew that that bringing things into the light eliminates any potential future hold, so he shared this experience with his management team. A different type of wisdom I think.

A short while later then, I was made redundant.

With a new house lease and now no job, there was an opportunity for a fresh story!

All good things come to an end

Every cloud has a silver lining

<u>Meggs Management Ltd</u>

I decided to pay for professional local advice and followed up a good friend's recommendation for a Firm of Accountants to help me set up my own limited company. Having been in management accounting for so long, and then in voluntary work too, my technical and tax expertise was seriously out of date.

One's own boss, back to being local

Within a couple of weeks' of my redundancy, I secured a temporary contract at a small Academy chain to implement a new accounting package. Hastings Academies Trust needed to implement a new accounting system. My interview was with the Head of Finance, with a follow up chat with the Director or Resources. I assumed that the Director of Resources role was subordinate to her Head of Finance position, still unsure why, and so was possibly overly relaxed at this point. Taking this as a supreme measure of confidence maybe, I was appointed for the five month implementation project.

I was desperate for work, and hoping that something would come up that wasn't in London. The train journey was expensive, unreliable and would add a couple of hours each way to the working day.

I capitalised on their need too and insisted that I would fulfil the project requirements, but only had four days a week to offer, being committed to Fridays already. They didn't need to know that I had yet to secure any international development or charity work yet! Seeing as I was now setting up my own contracting company, I decided that it would be done on my own terms. From now on, "normal work" would be done Monday through Thursday or 80% FTE (full time equivalent) enabling me to devote, notionally at least, 20% of my time to the work and projects I was really most interested in.

My very first day there and the Head of Finance arrived back in the office in tears, apparently not for the first time. That didn't bode well I thought.

A temporary Management Accountant was also brought in. A short while later, both the head of Finance, and the new Management Accountant, resigned, on the same day. They both gave reasonable reasons for exiting of course, but they both also confided in me that they couldn't work there anymore. Senior staff had set a culture that these professionals simply would not put up with.

I was asked to stay on, no surprise. I presented my accounting package findings, and quickly in order to meet their ever pressing deadline. The Director didn't like the apparent lack of choice in my report. I increasingly perceived that I was working for a detail freak and micro manager. One can move quickly, or, one can move with a lot of detail and research the entire market. Generally, in my experience, most accounting packages, of which there are many, will do the job.

I organised the office move, which was obviously in my skill set, to our new offices in the refurbished school. I then recruited a Temporary Accounts Assistant to see us through year end, accepting that they were in no way ready to implement a change of accounting package just yet.

I also volunteered to stay on to manage the Finance team whilst they recruited a new Head of Finance. I did this, and did it well I think, taking us through a smooth year end, unlike their previous year. I told them I would take on the Head of Finance role, so long as I could continue to do the job in four days a week, which I'd been doing for a year now already. They refused my offer. Having proved that I could everything they wanted over the course of the previous year, they now insisted more of my time was required to do the same.

They then appointed a new FD. He was escorted off the premises within a week. He was blatantly rude, sexist and manipulative. How he got through the interview was a mystery, apparently he was charming! They then recruited another temporary, less qualified and more expensive replacement. I found out that they'd gone through multiple Finance Heads, the average one lasting six months, over the past few years. The Chair of Governors, about a week before I left, and in my first ever conversation with him, asked whether I'd stay on. Too late and too cheap.

Not all Academies are the same

My one day a week role

Sierra Leone, continued

Joule Africa contracted me for a few days over a couple of months, which was insurance on their part, in case stuff I knew was needed! Of course it was. I knew this would be short lived and basically just passing over my knowledge but I needed the income! It also started an invoice sequence list for my fledgling company.

It's a joy to remain connected to Joule Africa, for two reasons. Their raison d'etre is to bring electricity to one of the poorest nations on the planet, and to have a sound, profitable, business model in doing so. The project has gone through a number of changes in London and Freetown, but has recently signed the final paperwork in order to commence the building and operating of the hydro-electric dams. It's going to happen, it's going to make a massive difference, and I was somehow able to play a part right at the start. Joule also rewarded their staff with shares, of which I have a number. My hope is that these shares might plug the very significant hole in my pension planning, the one that several years of voluntary work creates, and miraculously contribute towards what could look like an almost normal pension plan.

Sierra Leone, again

Completely coincidentally, a charity I'd come across in Harpenden was working in Freetown and they needed several years' worth of accounting work doing. Again, it was a connection with a person, that lead to numbers and details being exchanged, that resulted in a phone call years later. I was back on the plane, bus, boat, taxi again to Sierra Leone. The FCO guidance, which one sort of has to read, especially if you have travel insurance, suggests there are no safe ways to get from the airport to Freetown. You are required to make your own assessment of risk and choose appropriately.

I sat on the very small boat that takes you from the dock to the airport private coach stop, alongside the British Ambassador. He recalled arriving some ten years earlier and carrying his case on his head out into waste deep water to catch the boat. The first thing his team did was to re-build the wooden jetty. The British had been there all through this time. The Americans, now it was made safe for them, were beginning to start flights again. They were definitely only there for the money, I was proud to be British again, for doing the right thing, even when it's tough and thankless.

I think it's a truism that if you are known for doing things for free, and for doing it professionally, people trust you to deliver paid work too. In fact it almost serves as a reference when people don't know you too well.

Long days, with and without the generator and a/c were followed by sweaty nights. There was a small room above the workshop, not the bijoux guest house I'd been used to staying in. No security, no cook, no driver, no car even. This was helping the hard way and I was truly impressed with this charity. It was a husband and wife couple who had determined to make a difference and had bank-rolled a start-up garment factory with a training centre and youth employment facility. This was gradually turning itself into a profitable and standalone entity, by winning uniform contracts with some of the many mining and security companies in Sierra Leone. Despite the dangers and concerns they still persisted with frequent visits, training and support. Recently through the Ebola crisis, they managed to feed all the staff and their local community and not a single member got sick. They had no income during that season, except that which he sent out from the UK. And they still had to battle local prejudice and corruption every step of the way.

He'd nearly drowned on one occasion on the little airport ferry-boat, being battered in a storm as they fought their way across the largest natural harbour in Africa.

Bravery to my mind is still doing the right thing, when it's dangerous, when you might be scared, when it's neither convenient nor safe.

In resolving the several years of accounting transactions, they were a few differences in our debtors and creditors. Apparently, there, many organisations historically don't have either double entry or computerised records. What the supplier said we owed, we owed, if we even attempted to pay the extra it would unravel and open up all sorts of unwanted attention. Likewise taxes. If we challenged what they said we'd likely be shut down. The local electricity company had already tried that once, despite him having receipts for every invoice they'd paid!

Switzerland, to a different charity

Another email, this time from someone we met a couple of times in Switzerland. SwissLeg, and SwissLimb, was the practical result of a Master's in Business Administration that Roberto had taken. His professor challenging him to translate a theoretical concept into reality. He and his two colleagues only went and did it. They created a cheap and quick artificial prosthetic leg for amputees and victims of war, took it to the Swiss Government for sponsorship and set up a clinic in Jordan helping victims of the Syrian conflict. They wanted some assistance with some Guardian ® sponsored business event in London and then I flew out to help them get their accounting and reporting set up. The real benefit I delivered was probably the mentoring discussions about how to manage difficult colleagues and business partners! My now many years of experience made me a little more skilled in this regard. They are now expanding and working in other conflict areas, bringing much needed relief for the mostly innocent victims left behind. Currently they have operations in Jordan, Tanzania and Uganda.

Mrs M did join me for that trip; they were based in Lugano not far from Lake Como. The work was relatively straightforward, the company easy and the few nights away by Como one of my best business trips ever.

Nepal (five14.com)

We'd connected with a dear American couple back in Colorado, I'd paid particular attention to his opening introductory talk, primarily because he talked about using his motorbike to get around Nepal and Tibet, as it was the only way they could physically travel. They recalled the first car being delivered, on bamboo poles, there weren't yet any paved roads for it to be driven on.

These were the people involved in practical ways to help stop sex trafficking amongst the young girls in the remote Nepali villages. Being crude for a moment, Nepali women have lighter skin and that's deemed desirable, especially the further south in India you are.

We had kept in loose touch over the years and had seen the evolution of their business online. I knew that I could help at some stage, and wanted to see what they had accomplished. Eventually, my offer of help coincided with their need for assistance in some particular areas and so we organised a visit. I needed a break, and he for sure needed one, and so we hatched a plan; I'd employ my friend for a few days to travel around Nepal by motorbike, before spending a few days in the office, organising the accounting and technical administrative side of the organisation.

This was at last a proper adventure. We rented an old Honda XR250 for Mick and I ended up with a Royal Enfield. The first day was spent riding around Kathmandu to acclimatise me to the "rules" of Nepalese roads. These are (1) there aren't any rules except for (2) biggest has priority, always. I found this truly fun, in a masochistic dangerous way. The hardest traffic habit to cope with, especially being western, is that out here an indicator, if used at all, means a turn, although it could be to both sides and not necessarily the side that's flashing.

We attempted to ride out north east to a bridge that connects to China, one where you can, if lucky, cross briefly into Tibet and back.

There had been floods and landslides in this region several months earlier and the team there had been part of the local relief effort. Food and blankets were taken to the villages and handed over to the Elders. A bridge had broken with the landslide, and this had created a dam, backing up behind it creating a lake which swallowed the entire area. Houses and people were drowned and the area almost wiped away. Now, months later, the road was still an almost impassable track cut into the mountainside debris. Amazingly, some traffic, mainly larger trucks and smaller motorbikes, was getting through, but it was a hugely challenging process. After battling the track for a while without making much progress, we decided that we wouldn't make the border in time for evening and so we turned around half way up the pass.

The next day we took a different route to a border crossing to the north. After some truly dramatic roads just outside the city, smooth tarmac lulled me into a false sense of security. Turning off to another unsigned main road we rode ever upwards. In the distance below I could see people by the river-side. Zooming in the camera lens, it seemed to be a burial party. The custom is to place the dead on a pyre, set light to it and push it off down river. Poverty means that there wasn't always enough wood to burn the body and so they'd fall in the river. Local stories abound of human-fed monster catfish that could eat people. I thought it was a story until one of TV's monster fish documentaries I watched several months later at home!

Mick, my host and biking buddy for the trip, spoke Nepali badly, well in his opinion. He maintained that in speaking poorly, people would always try and help, and that asking people for help opened up friendship and assistance in a remarkable way. I watched him in action. People would gather round and help and point and offer to help and they'd laugh at his poor pronunciation and the world was truly a better place for a few moments. Mick was right.

We arrived at the last border town. Those at the start of the long treks were hiring the local porters, Sherpa and the like.

Nepalese thoughts towards their neighbours to the north weren't always warm. Poorer people exist in tribal groups. Modern country borders are often political, not tribal. Their relatives with less freedom to the north were part of their extended and now disconnected wider family. Ethnicity and culture and country is a fascinating concept for study. The UN might recognise China, Tibet and Nepal. Local people in that border town, especially if they do not have a passport, would understand Sherpa, Larke, Siar and Ghorka. Our young Burmese friends described themselves as being from the Chin tribe, who happened to spread across the countries we would recognise as Burma, India and Bangladesh. Geopolitics; I digress.

Some friendly locals pointed us to the only hotel in town that had western toilets and we were fixed for the night. The land lady's homemade "whisky" warmed our insides as the night fell.

We so very nearly blagged our way across the border for a photograph and hand shake. This appeared likely until a senior Chinese official arrived the other side and everything got very serious. Mick was on his usual good form, having ridden through multiple and increasingly armed military checkpoints until we found ourselves at the border with China. His "methodology" was to arrive, make loud gestures and greetings, and start to take helmets off and to shake hands. Their usual response was to see we were crazy foreigners and wave us through!

Our ride back was memorable, I now knew exactly what to expect from washed out roads; rock slides, terrifying drop offs, waterfalls washing over the road into the valley below, and pot holes you could fall into. The exhaust fell off the Enfield, which I strapped to the seat with some string. At the next town a local mechanic fixed it back on again and would take no payment.

I then spent a couple of days in the office, talking accounting, taxes, record keeping and the like. This just helped them move forwards one more step. Fantastic people, great project, wonderful country.

I get to play a tiny, helping role and, sometimes, to see it in action

Part time FD roles always mean more hours than you want

I took another call. I began to realise that once you gain a reputation within a particular field, you don't have to "do" marketing. I had finally arrived to a season where work finds you! This time another acquaintance from our time in Harpenden. He had an owner managed, but friend financed, African Telecoms Company, and needed "a bit of help". Well, that's how he described things.

I had already structured my working week to be four days long, informing those who asked, that as I was already connected to and committed to a number of charity and development projects. When I took the call, I had the time allocated. Although not a "development" fit, at least it was paid project consultancy work and invoices for Meggs Management Ltd.

The negotiation was an example of who holds power in any given encounter. I actually needed the money, and so when he said that he'd prefer to pay a monthly fee, irrespective of what work I did. I took it. I had yet to learn that although I had agreed to work one day a week, for him, I was now his FD. Of course, he and the company worked seven days a week, and being an owner managed business, work started and finished depending on when he was awake.

The train journeys to North London soon ceased their charm. If all the connections worked well, it would take two and a half hours door to door, each way. Somehow, despite living so far away, I was often the first to arrive at the office, but they'd all work on late. My Fridays started to feel very long indeed. Matters were not helped by receiving emails all times of the day, every day, to which he wanted immediate replies.

The business was, by some technical assessments, insolvent. It made continual small losses and only funded its operations by extending its African supplier payments a little more each month. He'd had friends invest as shareholders, then borrowed money from business associates in South Africa and then later had borrowed yet more from other friends and family. On top of the supplier debt, it was getting on for a million pounds. Thankfully, partly to less precise and efficient accounting at the African end, and partly as our business was a relatively minor proportion, the increasing supplier debt wasn't being noticed. It felt like a house of cards, just waiting for the wind to blow.

Suggestions I had, about proper accounting and debt management, were ignored or rebuffed. He had this unwavering optimism that eventually everything would work out. I suppose every small business owner does. They have to. Until it doesn't of course and I imagine that the high profile successful business one hears about, are just the few that do survive.

The travel took its toll. Despite my best efforts, what was still needed in the short term was basic accounting in order to submit accounts to Companies House. To help a friend from being fined as a Director, I rolled my sleeves up and, even though I dislike having to do it, I took to trying to populate an accounting system with proper records. What they'd been using was a rolling excel cash flow model, with no direct links to any form of "proper" accounting. I sacrificed weekends and Easter holidays to accomplish the filing. They paid lip service to the work I had done, but I felt they'd not really understood the service I'd provided at all. I spent the next year trying to convince him to employ a book-keeper and attempting to oversee the input into Sage. Next year-end soon loomed and I was yet again doing exactly the same work to help a friend out. My "friendship" felt a little stretched.

I did try to pull myself out, feeling like the situation was never going to resolve itself, unless something significant happened. I became much more direct with my reviews, especially surrounding solvency and duties as a Director under law. I declined his offer of a Directorship, especially as there was no remuneration. I was there simply to provide legitimacy to the company structure. I said I would reduce my contract so that he had cash to pay for other staff, he met with this "but you are of so much value to me, I need you around". I think my only value, in the end, was that I was able to be seen as a Director in his business meetings, as his only other director choice was barred from serving in that capacity! I have now been offered two directorships, both offers came from soon to be or technically insolvent companies.

Several potential buyers came and went. There was a huge effort to create documentation and business plans and prepare for meetings. Shares were offered, incentives to help see him through a sale process. However, when an offer to acquire his business did eventually materialise, I was casually fired in the two minute walk to the station. I'd just finished working the week-end away from home to get things ready for filing his accounts.

I'd engaged professional help to advise him on the various tax issues involved in the quite complex company sale. He admitted that he felt stupid in front of the new owners for paying for two sets of financial advice. So he let me go. That was that, two years, hard work and stress and emotional energy, wasted? It did however pay the rent.

Still learning life lessons in my fifties!

The journeying continues

Remarkably, I received a call that same week from Mango; would I be interested to hear about a part time, up to one day a week, position, working for an Egyptian based refugee agency. It seemed too good to be true. I had a skype interview with the Cairo based CEO and that was it, barely any time to breathe, and I was the Finance Consultant for a significant and effective overseas NGO.

St Andrew's Refugee Services, based out of a local church set up in 1908, has substantial income, by local standards, and hundreds of employees many of whom are or were refugees themselves. Through them, thousands of mainly African refugees are helped, counselled, fed and educated. This was a real role.

The work was complex but manageable. It was more convenient to have the oversight of the accounting, and the reporting to the various donor agencies, handled from the UK. The biggest challenge for me, and anyone in my role, is the way that every funder requires a different report, even the core input data is basic and the same. One individual cost item, or one employee, can be split and allocated across several different funders using different formulae!

The CEO's ability to win more funding meant that the scale quickly more than doubled! I was now working week-ends and evenings, using up holiday and wearing myself out! I resigned, before things became too much. If you work for long enough, you see patterns repeat themselves. I knew that sooner or later, my ability to service the work they needed would worsen. I had four days a month, the volume of work now meant they needed twice that. They could recruit someone with significantly more time and I'd oversee a transition process over several months and they would then be set for the next stage of their work. I remain impressed and amazed at the scale and impact and of their activities and the measurable outcomes. I played my part for the time I was involved.

One of the challenges in Cairo, at this time, or rather, in these times, is the prevailing attitudes and tensions worldwide between different faiths and cultures. Rhetoric about foreigners and foreign cultures would occasionally be raised and lowered, almost as a deliberate political device. Just like in George Orwell's book 1984, having a distant vague enemy means the focus is drawn away from local problems. Although this charity had been around as a local entity for a century or so, it would still become the focus for drive-by shooting target practice, as and when anti-foreign rhetoric was raised.

I received another email and then a call, from a different Middle Eastern charity, mainly funded from the UK. I was intrigued and went for a follow up meeting. Without going into too much detail, it was a project I eventually declined to be a part of. Sometimes we read in the news that some foreign head of state is having a crackdown on foreign NGOs and we all shake our heads in disapproval. Let's just say that from time to time, there's more going on than we can see.

Employed again; a positive Academy experience

The short term contract invitations kept coming but weren't enough to pay the bills by themselves. Actually most of them I continued to do for free anyway. They were great organisations doing amazing things and I wanted to help in any way I could.

An interim Finance role at another School came up, again through Hays, and I applied. They gave me a proper technical test, and required a presentation to a panel. Fortunately for me, they used the same historic and rubbish accounting system as I'd seen in the other schools. I knew how to extract the data, create a decent looking report. Crucially, I also knew from experience what the numbers meant and didn't mean.

I casually joked that "I didn't expect the Spanish Inquisition" when I walked in to the small office with five senior staff sat the other side of the conference table. I smiled inwardly at my own joke, finding it even funnier that only one of the five member panel were laughing at my attempt at humour. I kept my serious but confident face on. I've grown enough not to worry too much in these situations any more. I did however, make them all smile when I delivered my presentation. They asked how come I knew so much about their school, as I'd nailed so many of the issues they were facing without them mentioning them. The role was mine, when could I start?

Fortunately for me, my predecessor had done such a bad job with the finances, that whatever I did was met with gratitude and sighs of wonder. Here, I was met with a blank canvas, literally. There were almost no accounting files to review, except for the auditor prepared annual statements. This was a truly novel experience. The real change for me, was seeing a school run by a mature, competent, and happy and friendly leadership team. Working here was a joy.

My predecessor, in the historic "School Business Manager" role, had overseen Finance, Premises, HR and IT. However, it was apparent that in the area of finance, they were seriously out of their depth. My assessment fluctuated between harsh criticism and sympathetic understanding. Local Education Authorities, before Academies, didn't want higher level accounting input, likely interpreting this as interference. All the proper accounting tasks were performed at a central level and only the daily transactional elements were dealt with locally. They weren't expected or encouraged to be much more than clerks, at least in the Finance dept. This was one area where all of a sudden, Academies had to change and up their game.

The school had failed to meet its statutory financial deadlines in the last couple of years. So, coming in with my proper accounting experience, it was relatively easy to chart a path to success.

I created a simple month end procedure, a set of easy to read financial statements, produced monthly reports and set up a diary system to ensure that all the deadlines were met. I produced the same reports every month and explained the variances and set up budgets that we were able to manage. I'm not saying it was all that easy, but accounting practices and routines are all pretty much the same, whatever organisation or country one is in.

The meetings to present to Governors started off very tense indeed. They had felt as though they'd been kept in the dark before and indeed they had no real access to anything meaningful from a finance perspective. These events then went on for hours into the evening and could be a little confrontational. Gradually though, confidence grew, deadlines were met, meetings got shorter, and order was created. I even created budgets that they felt confident with.

The contract became permanent and eventually lead to an employed position. The freedom and flexibility that a contractor has was offset by security and stability for this new season.

Do the simple things well, Accounting is not rocket science

Closing thoughts

At the age of fifty three, I've been doing this accounting thing for some thirty five years. The lessons I've relayed in this book arise time and time again, truly there is nothing new under the sun.

These observations, mostly learned the hard way, are likely universal truths, and I would have valued someone telling me these, when I was in my youth and could have used them.

As I say to my boys, if you can learn from my mistakes, you can save yourself both time and pain!

I suspect though, that much like my sons, you'll ignore these truths, and realise, only in hindsight, that they were indeed of value.

My hope is that yes, the stories might be fun to read, but, especially as an Accountant, you realise that the entire world is open to you. It's a big exciting planet and your skills can take you right around it. It has for me.

Enjoy.

The sea is big and dangerous and ought to be tackled by those competent to do so, really

The list of things about your accounting career you won't get taught but when you are older you will wish you had been

- _Pronunciation is actually important – Mum was right after all_
- _If you don't plan, you'll end up going where the current takes you_
- _Healthcare is good business, people equals healthcare_
- _Everyone is weird, including you!_
- _Your best chance of a pay rise is to switch jobs and aim up_
- _You have a few weeks in your new job to live up to the expectations you created in your interview! Use that time wisely_
- _You have to get along with your co-workers, not like them._
- _Never trust a prospective employer who invites you to the interview at a hotel_
- _It really is all about who you know_
- _Starting a pension plan early is wisdom indeed_
- _Americans value loyalty and deference rather too highly_
- _Aspiring Accountants, learn to quote your source!_
- _Ask yourself about the values that drive a company_
- _A foreign language means a higher salary_
- _A single sheet of paper, that is how you manage a billion dollar company_
- _Corporate culture is a real thing_
- _The French like the French_
- _Connections & coincidences make the world work_
- _Project roles are exciting_
- _Roche has very low staff turnover, Roche is successful_
- _Plans are what you can achieve, set your Dreams much higher_

- *Generosity blows people away, and once you embrace it, is really fun*
- *Organisations have informal communication, countries too*
- *Time is indeed relative*
- *Water someone else's garden and trust that someone will water yours*
- *Middle class sports still open doors*
- *Try and understand your own culture through another's eyes, don't judge theirs until you've lived it*
- *Reverse "culture shock" is a real thing*
- *Travelling with families is much harder, but can be more rewarding*
- *The Public Sector is not the same as the Private Sector, not by a long way*
- *Islanders really do think differently*
- *If you're not fulfilled it shows*
- *Be deliberate about keeping hold of your dreams*
- *Invest in friendships – consciously & deliberately*
- *Humour is universal, but it is also very cultural*
- *If you are reading this, you really are part of the 1%*
- *India, it is very different*
- *Sometimes, you simply have to let go, and swim with the tide*
- *Values & Principles versus Rules & Laws*
- *Having a clear vision is key*
- *For your career, being deliberate and focused is crucial*
- *Don't trust anyone who says "don't worry it'll be easy"*
- *Toilets, common to all man-kind*
- *Business culture is still a culture to be learned*
- *Help is always close by*
- *The Swiss do things well, very well indeed.*
- *Presentation is crucial*
- *From rags to riches – it still happens*

- *Some coincidences you simply couldn't make up*
- *Accountants aren't perceived as voluntary workers*
- *Relationships, important*
- *What's your own attitude to risk? Are you happy with that answer?*
- *Never be too proud to accept instruction, even when you are expert*
- *Accounting principles are universal*
- *All good things come to an end*
- *Every cloud has a silver lining*
- *Part time FD roles always mean more hours than you want*
- *You get to play a helping role in charities*
- *Keep learning life lessons as you get older*
- *Do the simple things well, Accounting is not rocket science*
- *But it is perceived that way, and that's why you'll earn the big bucks!*

What doesn't kill you...?

Alternative book titles

An accounting book with no accounting – by Andrew Meggs

I am privileged to know a great number of people around the world, many of whom I call friends. Some of them have graciously tried to help me and suggested alternative titles for my book. I did like most of them, I know some very creative souls! So, enjoy these as I did.

Accountant Unplugged – by Marnie-Jane Agosta

2+2=5, Adventures in Accounting – by Pete Game

Unexpected Adventures in Accounting – by Nichola Dickson

It doesn't add up. Wild accounting – by Mark Jobbins

Making it Count. An Accountant's Account – by Robi Agosta

Unusual Ways to be an Accountant. Be an Accountant and See the World – by David Meggs

A Life That Doesn't Naturally Add Up – by Chris Williams

A book keeper's guide to the galaxy. I hadn't really taken that into Account. The accountants guide to world travel – by Richard Leakey

Double entry no exit. The story the numbers always tell. Cash in other lands – by Ian Soars

"Stuff I wish I knew when I was nineteen"

Made in the USA
Columbia, SC
14 October 2017